T5-BYN-315

A
ON THE
WILD SIDE
by NELSON ALGREN
author of THE MAN WITH THE GOLDEN ARM

Nelson Algren's
own book of
Lonesome
Monsters
Including stories by Saul Bellow, Joseph Heller, Thomas Pynchon, and the complete text of the famous short novel Among the Dangs by George P. Elliott
conversations with
NELSON ALGREN
by H. E. F. DONOHUE
NELSON
ALGREN
Notes from a Sea Diary:
Hemingway all the way

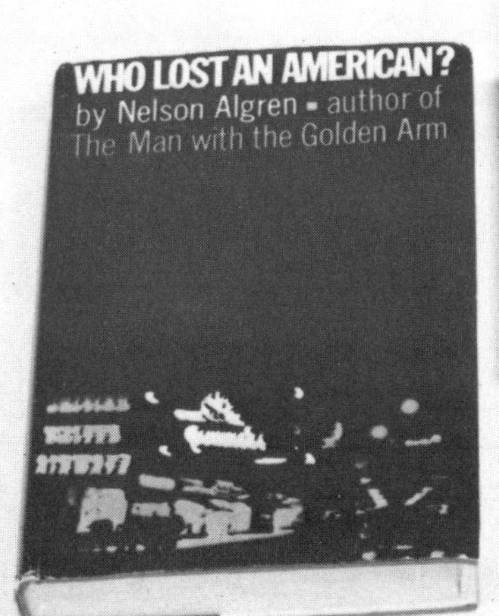

WHO LOST AN AMERICAN?
by Nelson Algren ▪ author of
The Man with the Golden Arm

NELSON ALGREN

A CHECKLIST

Sketch by Jean S. Poudrier

REN NELSON ALGREN NELSON ALGREN NEL

ALGREN NELSON ALGREN NELSON ALGREN

A CHECKLIST

Compiled by

Kenneth G. McCollum

Introduction

by

Studs Terkel

PUBLISHED BY GALE RESEARCH COMPANY, BOOK TOWER, DETROIT, 1973

First Printing

Book design and layout by Margaret Swanson Clark.

For Nelson Algren

Notes from a Sea Diary ALGREN PUTNAM

Nelson Algren's own book of Lonesome Monsters Bernard Geis Associates

DONOHUE conversations with NELSON ALGREN HILL AND WANG

A WALK ON THE WILD SIDE NELSON ALGREN FARRAR STRAUS AND CUDAHY

WHO LOST AN AMERICAN? Nelson Algren André Deutsch

CHICAGO: CITY ON THE MAKE NELSON ALGREN DOUBLEDAY

the MAN WITH THE GOLDEN ARM NELSON ALGREN DOUBLEDAY

NELSON ALGREN the neon wilder-ness

NELSON ALGREN Never Come Morning Harper

Somebody in Boots ALGREN VANGUARD

NELSON ALGREN: AN APPRECIATION

Nelson Algren may be the funniest man around. Which is another way of saying he may be the most serious. At a time when pimpery, lickspittlery and picking the public's pocket are the Order of the Day — indeed, officially proclaimed as Virtue — the poet (and Algren is certainly one of *them*) must play the madcap to keep his balance. And ours.

Unlike Father William, Algren does not stand on his head. He just shuffles along. His appearance is that of a horse player, who just got the news: he had bet her across the board and she came in a strong fourth. Yet, strangely, his is not a mournful mien. He's chuckling. You'd think he was the blue-eyed winner rather than the brown-eyed loser. And that's what's so funny about it. He *has* won. My hunch is his writings will be read long after acclaimed works of the Academe's darlings, yellowed on coffee tables, will be replaced by acclaimed works of other Academe's darlings. For in the spirit of a Zola and a Dreiser, he has captured a piece of that life "behind the billboards." Some comic, that man.

At a time when our values are unprecedently upside-down — when Bob Hope, a humorless multimillionaire is regarded as a funny man and a genuinely "funny" man, Richard Nixon, is regarded as Our President — Algren is something of a Gavroche. (Remember the Parisian gamin in *Les Miserables*? Hugo described him as irrepressible with life's delight in a world of whores, pimps and pickpockets. A pearl in a mud-society.)

"The hard necessity of bringing the judge on the bench down into the dock has been the peculiar responsibility of the writer in all ages of man." It was something Algren wrote in 1961, as an added preface to his prose-poem, *Chicago: City on the Make.* The original work had been composed a decade earlier. It's a responsibility to which he has been obstinately faithful. He's openhearted to Molly-O and Steffi and Margo and

Aunt Elly's "girl," who are forever up against it; who are forever in the pokey for turning a $5 trick with the wrong guy. He's mail-fisted to their judges, the Respectables, who turn a trick for no less than a hundred G's. So, too, this piece of writing from the same essay:

> "We have to keep Chicago strong
> and America mighty!" I heard His Honor
> proclaim before sentencing the girl
> with a record for addiction, "A year
> and a day! Take her away!"
>
> Blinking out of the window of
> an Ogden Avenue trolley at the
> sunlight she hadn't seen for almost
> a year, "I guess it was lucky I done
> that time," the girl philosophized,
> "Chicago still looks pretty strong
> and America looks mighty mighty."
>
> Still nobody seems to be
> laughing.

What Algren observed twelve years ago applies today in trump. And in that prose-poem, put down some twenty-odd years ago — and what odd years they've been! — the ring of a city's awful truth is still heard. Only louder. As with all good poets, the guy is a prophet.

It was no accident that he wrote *Man with the Golden Arm* so many centuries before posh suburban high schools fretted about junkies in their blue-eyed midst. The fate of Frankie Machine presaged adolescent hells to come. (Any similarity to the Otto Preminger-Frank Sinatra abomination of this classic is non-applicable because it *is* non-applicable.)

In *Never Come Morning,* Algren gave us Bruno, the doomed young jackroller. How different is he, the desperate city "ethnic," from the young black mugger? Law and Order is the cry today, as Algren so eloquently italicized the old poet's prophecy, "The slums will take their revenge."

Yet, this piece is supposed to be about Nelson Algren, the funny man. The antic sense is there, of course, in Dove Linkhorn, the innocent, of *A Walk on the Wild Side.* It's there in Frankie's colleague, Sparrow, the hapless shoplifter. It's there in Sometime-Willie, who always looked suspicious because he always suspected himself of one thing or another. It's there in Lost Ball Stahouska of the Baldhead A.C.'s. He was a caution, that one. Remember when his conscience bothered him because he shoved a baseball in his pocket, though he was unperturbed when cracking a safe with the help of three Chicago cops? As to the latter caper, Stahouska explained, "Oh, *everybody* does that." Again, you have it. Turning a $2 trick is a sin and prickly to the conscience. Turning a 20 Thou trick, that's something else again. Lost Ball, were he around today, could well appreciate the working of ITT, Penn Central, Lockheed and Howard Hughes. Recurring in all of Algren's works — novel, short story, poem ("Where have you gone, Sam The Jackal . . . ?") — is the theme of the rigged ball game. Offered in his unique lyric style, they are memorable.

Though today's literary mandarins treat the man with benign neglect — he has in the past twenty years become something of a non-person — he is highly regarded in unexpected quarters.

About a year ago, in the streets of London, I ran into a voluble Welshman. On learning I was an American — let alone a Chicagoan — he bought me a whiskey. I had no idea Americans were that popular with the people from Rhondda Valley. But it wasn't that at all. He could hardly wait to blurt it out. "You're an American. You must know of Nelson Algren." He proceeded, forthwith, to rattle off in mellifluous tongue, all of Algren's novels and short stories. On his discovering that I actually knew the man, he bought drink after drink after drink.

And on miner's pay, at that. How I got back to the hotel shall forever remain a mystery to me.

In New York, an old freight elevator man, a small, battered Irishman, whose one claim to immortality was an encounter with Fiorello LaGuardia, asked me, between floors, if I'd ever heard of a writer named Algren. He had read *The Neon Wilderness.* As far as I know, he owned no coffee table.

Recently, in a conversation with a woman on welfare, his name came up. It was she, not I, who introduced it. She had been reading one of his paperbacks. She had also been having her troubles with the Welfare Department and neighborhood cops. As far as I know, she owned no coffee table.

Maybe Nelson Algren's horses usually run out of the money. Maybe his luck at the poker table is not that good. Maybe he'll never be endowed by a university. But he has good reason to just shuffle along like a laughing winner. And he may be the funniest man around.

STUDS TERKEL
Chicago
March 1973

Compiler's Foreword

This checklist of Nelson Algren's work should provide the groundwork for a subsequent full bibliography. In the number-letter preceding the book entries, the number represents a separate *edition;* the letter indicates a printing within that edition. *Edition* means all the copies printed from a separate setting of type, including all the printings from that setting of type or plates made from that setting of type. *Printing* means all the copies printed *at one time* from the type or plates. Thus, 1B identifies the second time that the first setting of type went on the press. Those items I have not seen are marked with asterisks. Dates in brackets are not on the title pages.

The collations, such as $[1\text{-}21^8]$, indicate the number of bound gatherings in the book. For example, this collation indicates 21 gatherings with 8 leaves (16 pages) per gathering.

My chief debt is to Dr. Matthew J. Bruccoli of the University of South Carolina whose confidence in this effort made the compilation possible. Thanks are also due my wife, Judy, for her valuable editorial advice and expert secretarial assistance.

Kenneth McCollum
Fredericksburg, Virginia

Chronology

28 March 1909 — Nelson Ahlgren Abraham was born in Detroit, the son of a Scandinavian father and a Jewish mother.

1931 — Graduated in Journalism from the University of Illinois.

1931-1933 — Traveled the South and Southwest. Worked as migratory laborer in Texas.

1933 — Published short story titled "So Help Me" in *Story* magazine. The piece was noticed by Vanguard publishers who sponsored Algren's first novel.

1935 — Published *Somebody in Boots.*

1936 — Was married and went to work as a writer for the Chicago WPA.

1936-1939 — Worked periodically for the WPA.

1939 — Divorced. Was managing editor of *The New Anvil.*

1942 — Published *Never Come Morning.*

1942-1945 — Served with the Army in England and on the Continent.

1945 — Returned to Chicago.

1947 — Published volume of short stories, *The Neon Wilderness.*

1948 — Traveled through southern United States and Central America with French novelist, Simone de Beauvoir.

1949 — Published *The Man with the Golden Arm.* Traveled through Europe with Simone de Beauvoir.

1950 — Went to Hollywood to work on movie script for *The Man with the Golden Arm.*

1951 — Published *Chicago: City on the Make.*

1956 — Published *A Walk on the Wild Side.*

1960 — Traveled through Europe with Simone de Beauvoir.

1962 — Published *Nelson Algren's Own Book of Lonesome Monsters.* Set sail on an around-the-world trip aboard the freighter *Malaysia Mail.*

1963 — Published *Who Lost an American?*

1964 — Published, with H.E.F. Donohue, *Conversations with Nelson Algren.*

1965 – Published *Notes from a Sea Diary: Hemingway All the Way.*

1969 – Went as a journalist to Vietnam to cover the Chieu Hoi Program, an American endeavor to encourage enemy defectors.

1970-1973 – Worked on collection, *The Last Carousel.*

Note: Pennington Press of Chicago advertised *The World of Nelson Algren* in 1959. This was to be a book about Chicago by Algren; however, the Pennington Press went out of business before the book was published.

Dear Ken,
Paste this in your copy of Somebody in Boots.
It's the author's contract for that novel. If it doesn't offer the record-low in advances, then we'll have to wait to see what Harold Robbins gets for his next one—
best—
Nelson

COPY

September 14, 1933

Dear Mr. Abraham,

This letter will confirm the agreement we reached verbally yesterday afternoon. The Vanguard Press has advanced you $10.00 to finance you in writing your novel tentatively entitled THE GODS GATHER. We agree to advance you an additional $90.00 for this purpose, $30.00 to be paid immediately, $30.00 on October 15th and $30.00 on November 15th. In return for this, you agree to let us read, some time in December, the portions of your novel you have completed by then. If we feel that we then want to publish your novel when completed, we are to advance you an additional hundred dollars and you are to give us the completed manuscript on or before March 15, 1934.

The option hereby given us on this novel is based on the understanding that all advance payments are to be deducted from royalties, that royalties are to 10% on the first 5,000 copies sold and 15% on all copies sold above that sum; you are to receive 75% and the Vanguard Press 25% of the motion picture, talking picture and dramatic rights; all other rights are to be divided equally between you and the publishers. All other terms in connection with the publication of this novel are to be in accordance with our customary contracts.

Yours sincerely,

Mr. Nelson Algren Abraham
c/o Robert Andruss
2805 Creston Avenue
Bronx, New York

jh: mt

Approved

Nelson Abraham Algren
(signed)

I recall that, leaving N.Y. with a ten-dollar bill in my pocket and the assurance of $90.00 more, I could hardly conceal my satisfaction with my own shrewdness & I caught box car to Texas and never stopped congratulating myself all the way. I'd really put one over, I felt. N.

This agreement for *The Gods Gather* guaranteed Algren a munificent advance of $10. The manuscript was eventually submitted as *Native Son* and the title was changed by the publisher to *Somebody in Boots.*

Books

Somebody in Boots

A novel by Nelson Algren

The Vanguard Press · New York

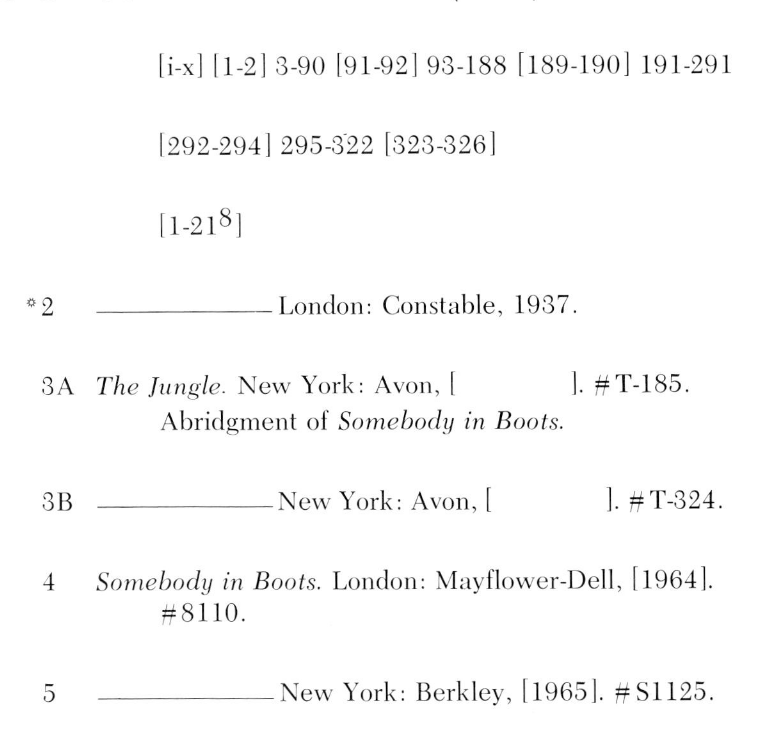

I. 1 SOMEBODY IN BOOTS (1935)

[i-x] [1-2] 3-90 [91-92] 93-188 [189-190] 191-291

[292-294] 295-322 [323-326]

[1-21^{8}]

*2 ——————— London: Constable, 1937.

3A *The Jungle.* New York: Avon, [ ]. #T-185.
Abridgment of *Somebody in Boots.*

3B ——————— New York: Avon, [ ]. #T-324.

4 *Somebody in Boots.* London: Mayflower-Dell, [1964].
#8110.

5 ——————— New York: Berkley, [1965]. #S1125.

NEVER COME MORNING

by

NELSON ALGREN

WITH AN INTRODUCTION BY
RICHARD WRIGHT

Harper & Brothers Publishers

NEW YORK AND LONDON

II. 1A NEVER COME MORNING (1942)

Copyright page: FIRST EDITION

[i-viii] ix-x [xi-xvi] 1-284 [285-288]

[1-19^8]

1B ______________ London: Neville Spearman, [1958].

2 ______________ New York: Avon, [1948]. #185. Revised and abridged by the author.

3 ______________ New York, Evanston & London: Harper & Row, [1963]. Colophon Book #CN15. With new preface by the author.

*4 ______________ London: Transworld, 1964. Corgi Book #FN1469.

5 ______________ New York: Berkley, [1968]. #N1583.

the neon wilderness

NELSON ALGREN

doubleday & co., inc., garden city, n.y. 1947

III. 1A THE NEON WILDERNESS (1947)

[1-17] 18-286 [287-288]. First page of each story is unnumbered.

[1-9^{16}]

Contents: "The Captain Has Bad Dreams," "How the Devil Came Down Division Street," "Is Your Name Joe?", "Depend on Aunt Elly," "Stickman's Laughter," "A Bottle of Milk for Mother," "He Couldn't Boogie Woogie Worth a Damn," "A Lot You Got to Holler," "Poor Man's Pennies," "The Face on the Barroom Floor," "The Brothers' House," "Please Don't Talk About Me When I'm Gone," "He Swung and He Missed," "El Presidente de Méjico," "Kingdom City to Cairo," "That's the Way It's Always Been," "The Children," "Million-Dollar Brainstorm," "Pero Venceremos," "No Man's Laughter," "Katz," "Design for Departure," "The Heroes," "So Help Me."

1B ______ Garden City: Doubleday, 1948.

2A ______ New York: Avon, [1949]. #222.
18 stories.

2B ______ New York: Avon, [ ]. #T-125.

3 ______ New York: Berkley, 1965. #S1103.
24 stories.

*4 ______ London: Deutsch, 1965

THE MAN WITH THE GOLDEN ARM

a novel by Nelson Algren

doubleday & company, inc., garden city, n.y., 1949

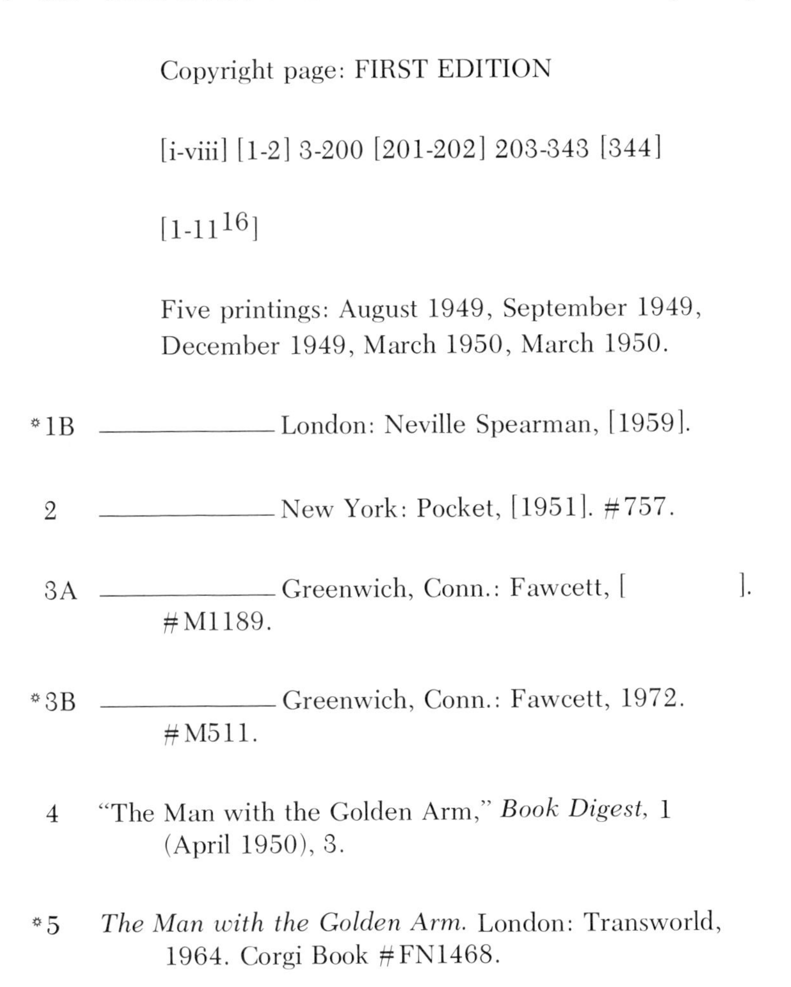

IV. 1A THE MAN WITH THE GOLDEN ARM (1949)

Copyright page: FIRST EDITION

[i-viii] [1-2] 3-200 [201-202] 203-343 [344]

[1-11^{16}]

Five printings: August 1949, September 1949, December 1949, March 1950, March 1950.

*1B ———— London: Neville Spearman, [1959].

2 ———— New York: Pocket, [1951]. #757.

3A ———— Greenwich, Conn.: Fawcett, [ ]. #M1189.

*3B ———— Greenwich, Conn.: Fawcett, 1972. #M511.

4 "The Man with the Golden Arm," *Book Digest*, 1 (April 1950), 3.

*5 *The Man with the Golden Arm.* London: Transworld, 1964. Corgi Book #FN1468.

chicago: city on the make

by Nelson Algren

DOUBLEDAY & COMPANY, INC. GARDEN CITY, NEW YORK, 1951

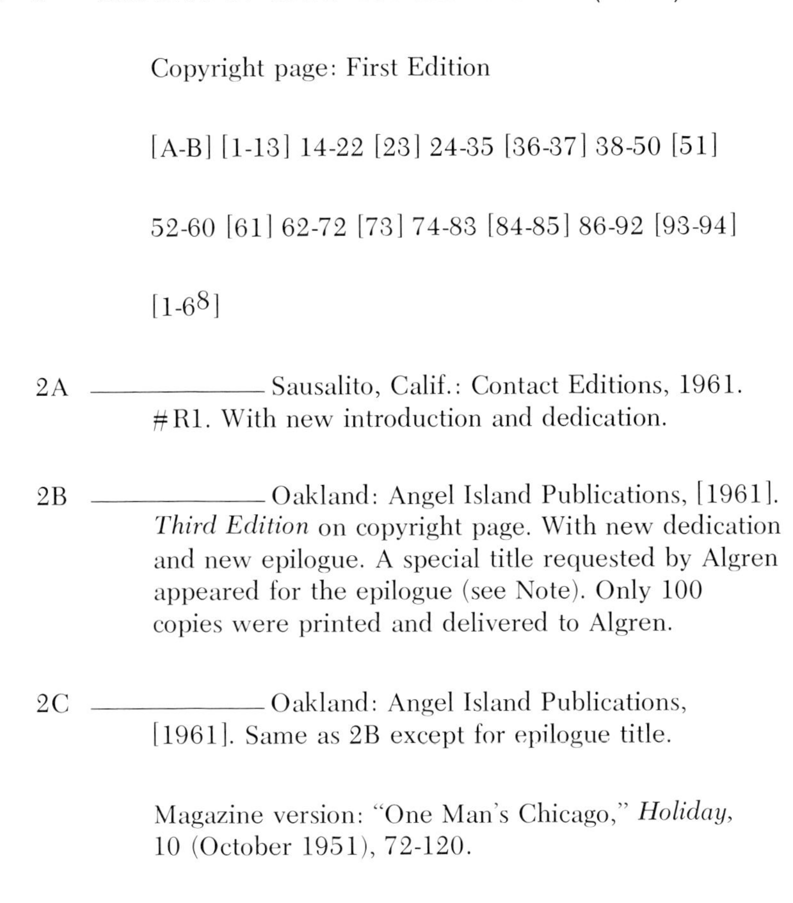

V. 1 CHICAGO: CITY ON THE MAKE (1951)

Copyright page: First Edition

[A-B] [1-13] 14-22 [23] 24-35 [36-37] 38-50 [51]

52-60 [61] 62-72 [73] 74-83 [84-85] 86-92 [93-94]

[1-6^{8}]

2A ———— Sausalito, Calif.: Contact Editions, 1961. #R1. With new introduction and dedication.

2B ———— Oakland: Angel Island Publications, [1961]. *Third Edition* on copyright page. With new dedication and new epilogue. A special title requested by Algren appeared for the epilogue (see Note). Only 100 copies were printed and delivered to Algren.

2C ———— Oakland: Angel Island Publications, [1961]. Same as 2B except for epilogue title.

Magazine version: "One Man's Chicago," *Holiday*, 10 (October 1951), 72-120.

Note: It seems that Algren originally titled the epilogue "Ode to Lower Finksville." After the manuscript was submitted, he decided to change the title to "Ode to Kissassville or: Gone on the Arfy-Darfy." The publisher considered this in bad taste and would not agree. Algren, however, would not back down.

An advertising executive served as arbitrator, and as a result Algren was personally furnished with 100 copies of the book in which the epilogue bore the title of his choice. The copies for sale contained the original title. An article by Robert Cromie from the 16 February 1968 *Chicago Tribune** described these incidents and was reprinted as an advertisement for the book.

*Robert Cromie, "Cromie Looks at Authors and Books," *Chicago Tribune,* Section 1 (16 February 1968), 23.

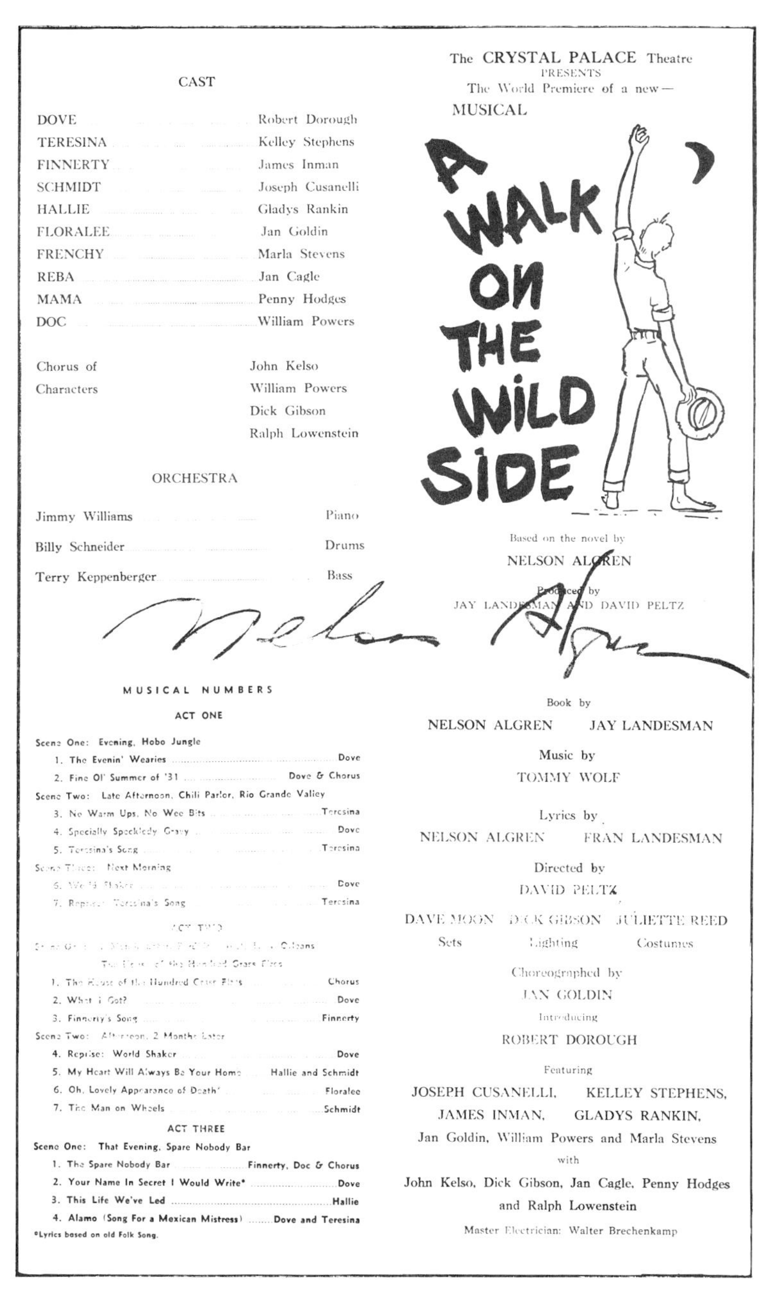

The CRYSTAL PALACE Theatre
PRESENTS
The World Premiere of a new—
MUSICAL

A WALK ON THE WILD SIDE

Based on the novel by
NELSON ALGREN

Produced by
JAY LANDESMAN AND DAVID PELTZ

CAST

DOVE	Robert Dorough
TERESINA	Kelley Stephens
FINNERTY	James Inman
SCHMIDT	Joseph Cusanelli
HALLIE	Gladys Rankin
FLORALEE	Jan Goldin
FRENCHY	Marla Stevens
REBA	Jan Cagle
MAMA	Penny Hodges
DOC	William Powers

Chorus of Characters: John Kelso, William Powers, Dick Gibson, Ralph Lowenstein

ORCHESTRA

Jimmy Williams	Piano
Billy Schneider	Drums
Terry Keppenberger	Bass

MUSICAL NUMBERS

ACT ONE

Scene One: Evening, Hobo Jungle
1. The Evenin' Wearies ... Dove
2. Fine Ol' Summer of '31 ... Dove & Chorus

Scene Two: Late Afternoon, Chili Parlor, Rio Grande Valley
3. No Warm Ups, No Wee Bits ... Teresina
4. Specially Speckledy Gravy ... Dove
5. Teresina's Song ... Teresina

Scene Three: Next Morning
6. World Shaker ... Dove
7. Reprise: Teresina's Song ... Teresina

ACT TWO

Scene One: [illegible] Orleans
The House of the Hundred Grass Flats
1. The House of the Hundred [illegible] ... Chorus
2. What I Got? ... Dove
3. Finnerty's Song ... Finnerty

Scene Two: Afternoon, 2 Months Later
4. Reprise: World Shaker ... Dove
5. My Heart Will Always Be Your Home ... Hallie and Schmidt
6. Oh, Lovely Appearance of Death* ... Floralee
7. The Man on Wheels ... Schmidt

ACT THREE

Scene One: That Evening, Spare Nobody Bar
1. The Spare Nobody Bar ... Finnerty, Doc & Chorus
2. Your Name In Secret I Would Write* ... Dove
3. This Life We've Led ... Hallie
4. Alamo (Song For a Mexican Mistress) ... Dove and Teresina

*Lyrics based on old Folk Song.

Book by
NELSON ALGREN JAY LANDESMAN

Music by
TOMMY WOLF

Lyrics by
NELSON ALGREN FRAN LANDESMAN

Directed by
DAVID PELTZ

DAVE MOON, Sets — DICK GIBSON, Lighting — JULIETTE REED, Costumes

Choreographed by
JAN GOLDIN

Introducing
ROBERT DOROUGH

Featuring
JOSEPH CUSANELLI, KELLEY STEPHENS, JAMES INMAN, GLADYS RANKIN,
Jan Goldin, William Powers and Marla Stevens
with
John Kelso, Dick Gibson, Jan Cagle, Penny Hodges and Ralph Lowenstein

Master Electrician: Walter Brechenkamp

Playbill for World Premiere of *A Walk on the Wild Side*, Crystal Palace Theater, St. Louis, 11 February 1960, courtesy of Ohio State University Libraries.

Nelson Algren

A WALK ON THE WILD SIDE

Farrar, Straus and Cudahy
NEW YORK

VI. 1A A WALK ON THE WILD SIDE (1956)

Copyright page: First printing, 1956

[i-vi] [1-2] 3-114 [115-116] 117-284 [285-286]

287-346

[1-11^{16}]

*1B ______________ London: Neville Spearman, [1957].

*2 ______________ Canada: Ambassador Books, 1956.

3 ______________ Greenwich, Conn.: Fawcett, [1963]. Crest #d496. Seven printings. Revised by the author.

4 ______________ London: Transworld, 1964. Corgi Book #FN1467.

Note: A musical version was premiered at the Crystal Palace, St. Louis, Missouri, on 11 February 1960. Book by Nelson Algren and Jay Landesman; lyrics by Nelson Algren and Fran Landesman. The program for this production contained 10 lyrics.

NELSON ALGREN'S
OWN BOOK OF

LONESOME MONSTERS

LANCER BOOKS, INC. • 26 WEST 47TH STREET • NEW YORK 36, N.Y.

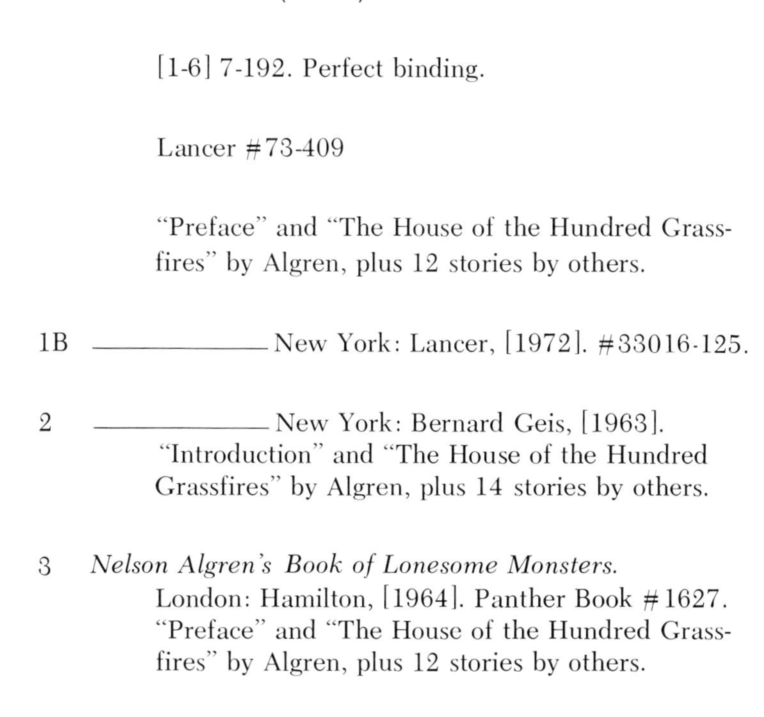

VII. 1A NELSON ALGREN'S OWN BOOK OF LONESOME MONSTERS (1962)

[1-6] 7-192. Perfect binding.

Lancer #73-409

"Preface" and "The House of the Hundred Grassfires" by Algren, plus 12 stories by others.

1B _____________ New York: Lancer, [1972]. #33016-125.

2 _____________ New York: Bernard Geis, [1963].
"Introduction" and "The House of the Hundred Grassfires" by Algren, plus 14 stories by others.

3 *Nelson Algren's Book of Lonesome Monsters.*
London: Hamilton, [1964]. Panther Book #1627.
"Preface" and "The House of the Hundred Grassfires" by Algren, plus 12 stories by others.

NELSON ALGREN

WHO LOST AN AMERICAN?

ANDRE DEUTSCH

VIII. 1 WHO LOST AN AMERICAN? (1963)

London, [1963].

[A-B] [i-vi] vii-viii [ix-x] 1-337 [338-340]

[1-11^{16}]

1A ———— New York: Macmillan, 1963.

2 ———— London: Mayflower-Dell, [1965].
#9535.

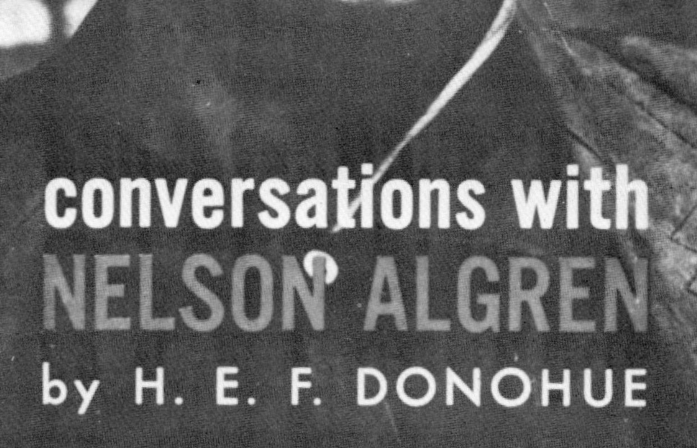
conversations with
NELSON ALGREN
by H. E. F. DONOHUE

IX. 1 BROCHURE FOR CONVERSATIONS WITH NELSON ALGREN (1964)

Cover title

[1-6]

Single leaf folded twice.

Note: The publisher issued this foldout six-page promotional piece containing excerpts from the book. Issued before October 1964.

CONVERSATIONS WITH Nelson Algren

BY H. E. F. DONOHUE

HILL AND WANG • NEW YORK

X. 1 CONVERSATIONS WITH NELSON ALGREN (1964)

Copyright page: First edition October 1964

[A-B] [i-vi] vii-ix [x] xi-xii [1-2] 3-98 [99-100]

101-167 [168-170] 171-191 [192-194] 195-243

[244-246] 247-333 [334-338]

[1-11^{16}]

2 ———————— New York: Berkley, [1965]. #S1134.

NOTES FROM A SEA DIARY:

Hemingway All The Way

NELSON ALGREN

G. P. Putnam's Sons, New York

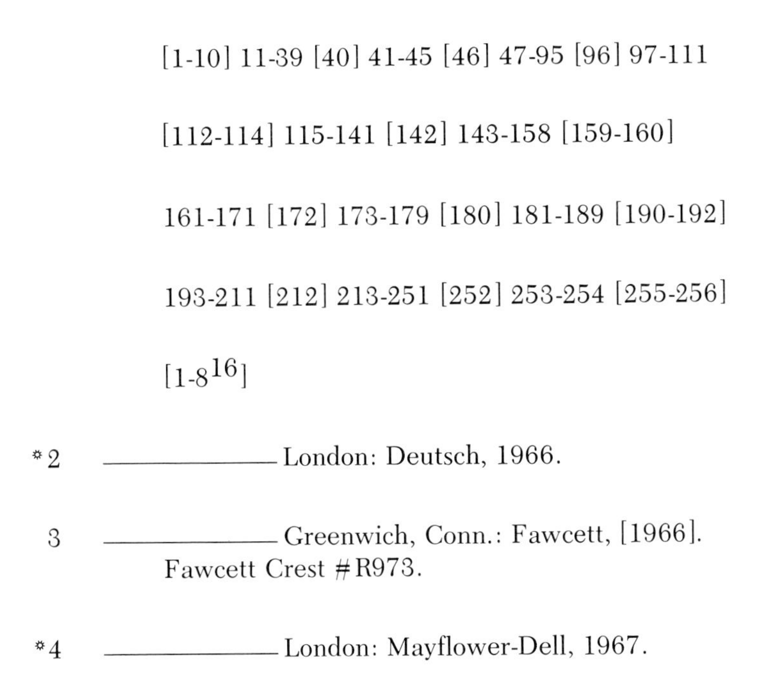

XI. 1 NOTES FROM A SEA DIARY: HEMINGWAY ALL THE WAY (1965)

[1-10] 11-39 [40] 41-45 [46] 47-95 [96] 97-111

[112-114] 115-141 [142] 143-158 [159-160]

161-171 [172] 173-179 [180] 181-189 [190-192]

193-211 [212] 213-251 [252] 253-254 [255-256]

[1-8^{16}]

*2 ______________ London: Deutsch, 1966.

3 ______________ Greenwich, Conn.: Fawcett, [1966]. Fawcett Crest #R973.

*4 ______________ London: Mayflower-Dell, 1967.

First Book Appearances

American Guide Series

GALENA GUIDE

Compiled and Written by

FEDERAL WRITERS' PROJECT (ILLINOIS)

Works Progress Administration

§

Sponsored by

THE CITY OF GALENA

1937

The *Galena Guide* was a collaborative Chicago WPA effort to which Algren contributed.

The *Galena Guide* was a collaborative effort by the Chicago WPA. There are varying opinions regarding the extent of Algren's contributions. The September 1971 *Serif* gives the impression that Algren was solely responsible for writing the book. Annotations in a copy owned by Matthew J. Bruccoli indicate that Algren may have written only one section. For further information on Algren's contributions to the *Galena Guide*, see articles by Bruccoli and Robert A. Tibbetts in the Fall 1972 *Serif*.

O. Henry Memorial Award Prize Stories of 1941, ed. Herschell Brickell. Garden City: Doubleday, Doran, 1941. "A Bottle of Milk for Mother."

Best American Short Stories 1942, ed. Martha Foley. Boston: Houghton, Mifflin, [1942]. "Biceps."

Modern Reading. London: Wells, Gardner, Darton, 1943. "The Captain is a Card."

* *Cross Section*. New York: Simon and Schuster, 1947. "Single Exit."

The Penguin New Writing, ed. John Lehmann. New York and London: Penguin, 1948. "The Heroes."

New World Writing. New York: New American Library, 1956. "Beasts of the Wild."

Writers at Work, ed. Malcolm Cowley. New York: Viking, 1958. Interview by Alston Anderson and Terry Southern.

* *Taboo.* Chicago: New Classics House, [1964]. "The Daddy of Them All."

Authors Take Sides on Vietnam, ed. Cecil Woolf and John Bagguley. New York: Simon and Schuster, 1967. Reply to questionnaire.

The True Story of Bonnie and Clyde: As Told by Bonnie's Mother and Clyde's Sister, ed. Jan I. Fortune. New York: Signet, 1968. "Introduction."

Works in Progress, No. 1. New York: Literary Guild, 1970. "Airy Persiflage on the Heaving Deep."

* *Focus/Media.* Scranton, Pa.: Chandler, 1972. "Otto Preminger's Strange Suspenjers." Later in *Chicago Sunday Sun-Times Midwest Magazine* (21 May 1972), 16.

Contents

Contents page of *Galena Guide*.
In the collection of Matthew J. Bruccoli.

Stories (First Magazine Appearances)

This issue of *Masses*, a socialist bimonthly published by the Progressive Arts Clubs of Canada, contained a prepublication excerpt from *Somebody in Boots.*

* "Forgive Them, Lord," *A Year Magazine,* Section II (1933), 144. This magazine was edited and published by J. Louis Stoll. The original plan was that it would be a quarterly; however, only two sections were published. If the magazine followed the normal sequence for quarterlies, then this would be the spring issue. Therefore, "Forgive Them, Lord" would be Algren's first piece published professionally; not "So Help Me" (August 1933) as previously believed.

"So Help Me," *Story,* III (August 1933), 3. This story of homeless vagabonds, previously believed to be Algren's first piece published professionally, is based on Algren's travels in the Southwest in the early thirties. It was through this story that Vanguard Press discovered Algren and advanced him money for the preparation of his first novel, *Somebody in Boots.*

"For the Homeless Youth of America," *Masses* (Toronto), 2 (March-April 1934), 4. This material is not a self-contained story, but rather an excerpt from *Somebody in Boots.* An interesting blurb appeared with the material announcing that it was taken "from his [Algren's] novel NATIVE SON." Algren chose this title which was subsequently changed by the publisher and which was later borrowed from Algren at the request of Richard Wright. The advance agreement from Vanguard listed the title as "The Gods Gather."

"If You Must Use Profanity," *American Mercury,* XXXI (April 1934), 430. Excerpt from *Somebody in Boots,* which Algren used as a separate story.

"Holiday in Texas," *The Anvil,* No. 6 (May-June 1934), 23.

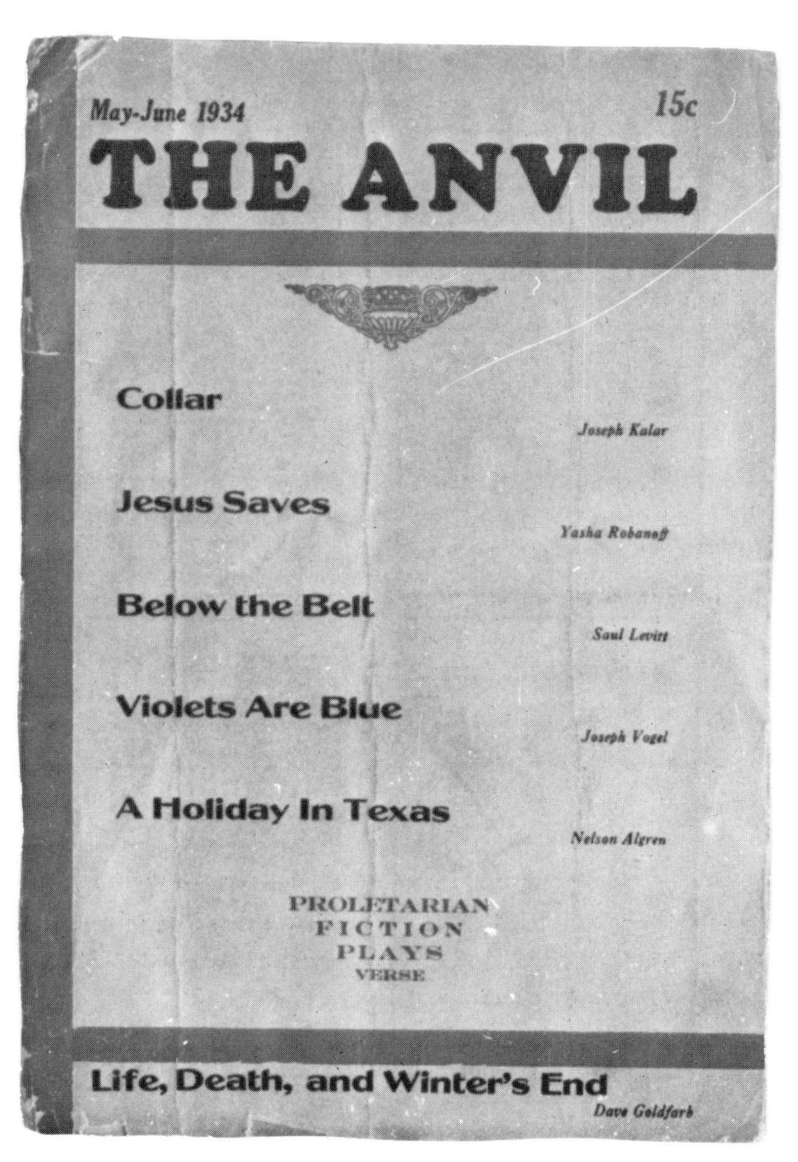
May-June 1934

15c

THE ANVIL

Collar

Joseph Kalar

Jesus Saves

Yasha Robanoff

Below the Belt

Saul Levitt

Violets Are Blue

Joseph Vogel

A Holiday In Texas

Nelson Algren

PROLETARIAN
FICTION
PLAYS
VERSE

Life, Death, and Winter's End

Dave Goldfarb

The Anvil, a socialist bimonthly, was edited by Jack Conroy in Moberly, Missouri. This issue contained an Algren story used as background for *Somebody in Boots.*

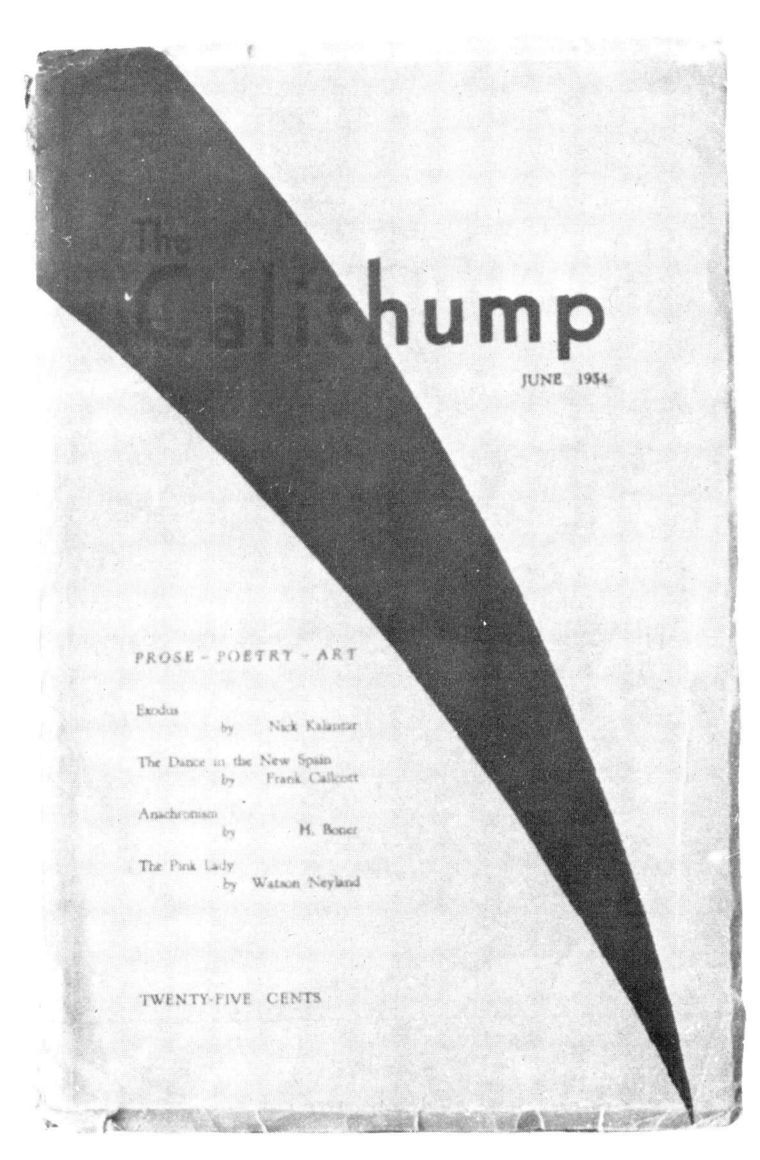

The June 1934 issue of *Calithump*, a monthly published in Austin, Texas, contained "Lest the Traplock Click."

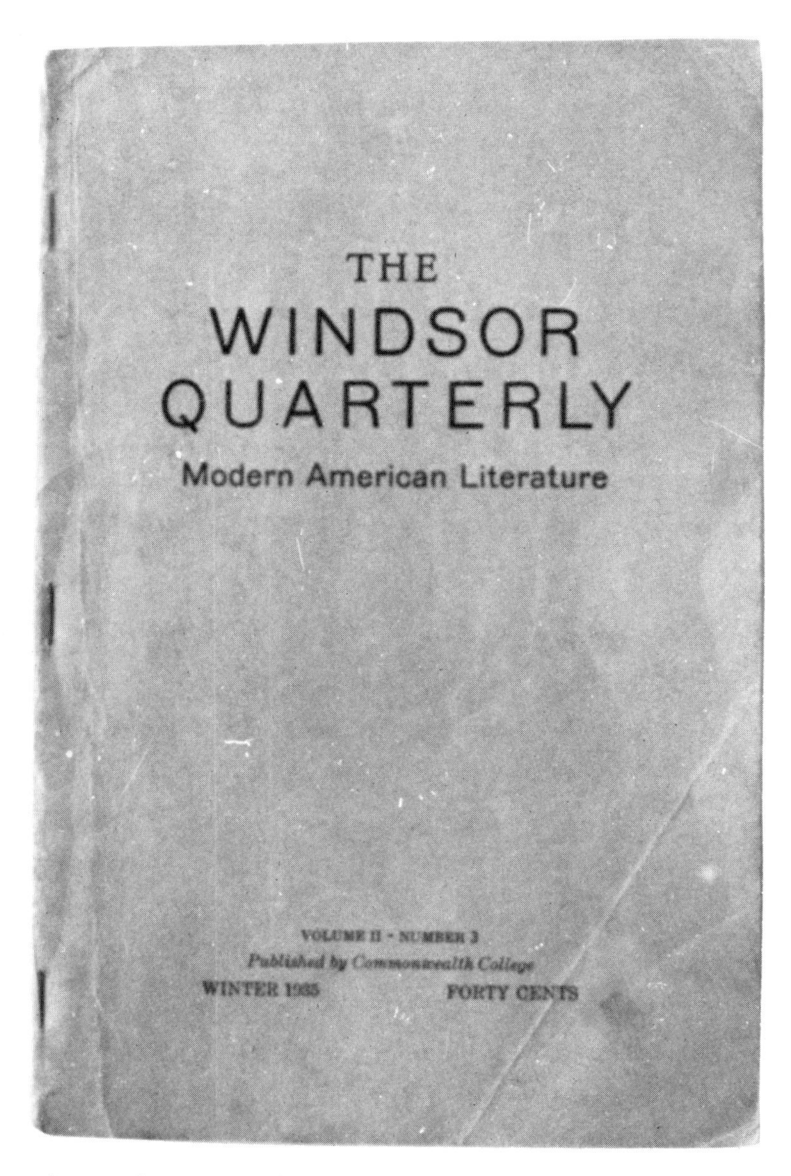

The Windsor Quarterly, published by Commonwealth College in Arkansas, was "doomed" by the publication of Algren's "Thundermug" in the Winter 1935 issue.

Commonwealth College Retreats

Commonwealth College admits sorrowfully that it has censored this issue of *The Windsor Quarterly*. "Thundermug," by Nelson Algren, was accepted for publication in this issue, was advertised, and was actually printed.

Many members of the Commonwealth College Association agree with the editor of the *Quarterly* that it is a powerful story. They urge that readers of the *Quarterly* secure a copy of *Somebody in Boots*, the novel of which "Thundermug" is a part, and read it to learn something new and vital about the world in which they live. *Somebody in Boots* will be published March 27 by The Vanguard Press.

But a few days before *The Windsor Quarterly* was to have been bound and mailed, Commonwealth was savagely attacked by the forces of reaction in the state of Arkansas. As this is written a drastic "anti-sedition" bill is pending in the Arkansas senate. The school is fighting for its life.

Because "Thundermug" violates ancient taboos, reactionary leaders in the state could have enlisted the support of thousands of fundamentalists, who otherwise are not much interested in a fight between Commonwealth and the share-croppers on one side and wealthy planters on the other. The fight for economic change is, of course, a fight for artistic freedom as well, but the school now has all the opposition it can take.

And so the school appears in the sorry role of censor and hopes that its liberal friends will understand and, in view of the desperate situation, will forgive this retreat.

Finally, we do not expect to be placed again in a position where it will be necessary to interfere with the editorial policy of *The Windsor Quarterly*.

Commonwealth College — Mena, Arkansas

Back cover of *The Windsor Quarterly*, Winter 1935.

Dear Ken,

This issue marked the end of the *Windsor Quarterly*, because of the story called Thundermug. This issue is one of a few the editor ran off secretly. The regular issue contained blank pages under the explanation: "CENSORED BY COMMONWEALTH COLLEGE." A tempest in a teapot, but it cost the editor her magazine. See her explanation on the back.

Did you know George Wallace was a student at Commonwealth at this time?

— Nelson

Nelson Algren's explanation of the "Thundermug" - *Windsor Quarterly* incident.

"Lest the Traplock Click," *The Calithump*, 1 (June 1934), 21.

* "Kewpie Doll," *The Anvil*, No. 7 (July-August 1934), 26.

"The Brothers' House," *Story*, 5 (October 1934), 22.

"A Place to Lie Down," *Partisan Review*, II (January-February 1935), 3. Edited excerpt from *Somebody in Boots.*

"Thundermug," *The Windsor Quarterly*, II (Winter 1935), 206.

* "Winter in Chicago," *The Anvil*, 2 (May-June 1935), 27.

"Biceps," *Southern Review*, 6 (1940-41), 713. This story was taken from *Never Come Morning*, and appeared as "A Bottle of Milk for Mother" in *O. Henry Memorial Award Prize Stories of 1941* and in *The Neon Wilderness.*

"Stickman's Laughter," *Southern Review*, 7 (1941-42), 845.

"The Captain is a Card," *Esquire*, XVII (June 1942), 50.

"He Swung and He Missed," *American Mercury*, 55 (July 1942), 57.

"The Children," *American Mercury*, 57 (September 1943), 310.

"How the Devil Came Down Division Street," *Harper's Bazaar*, No. 2789 (May 1944), 106.

"The Face on the Barroom Floor," *American Mercury,* 64 (January 1947), 26.

"The Captain is Impaled," *Harper's,* 199 (August 1949), 88.

"All Through the Night," *Playboy,* 4 (April 1957), 29.

* "Ding Dong, Tinkle Hinkle, the Finkified Lasagna and the Footnote King," *Dial,* 1 (Fall 1959), 125.

"God Bless the Lonesome Gas Man," *Dude,* 6 (March 1962), 11.

"The Moon of the Arfy Darfy," *Saturday Evening Post,* CCXXXVII (26 September 1964), 44.

"A Ticket on Skoronski," *Saturday Evening Post,* CCXXXIX (5 November 1966), 48.

"Home to Shawneetown," *Atlantic Monthly,* 222 (August 1968), 41.

"Decline & Fall of Dingdong-Daddyland," *Commentary,* 48 (September 1969), 69.

"Get All the Money," *Playboy,* 17 (June 1970), 82.

"Swan Lake Re-Swum," *Audience,* 1 (January 1971), 10.

"The Last Carrousel," *Playboy,* 19 (February 1972), 72.

"I Never Hollered Cheezit the Cops," *Atlantic Monthly*, 230 (October 1972), 93.

Poems

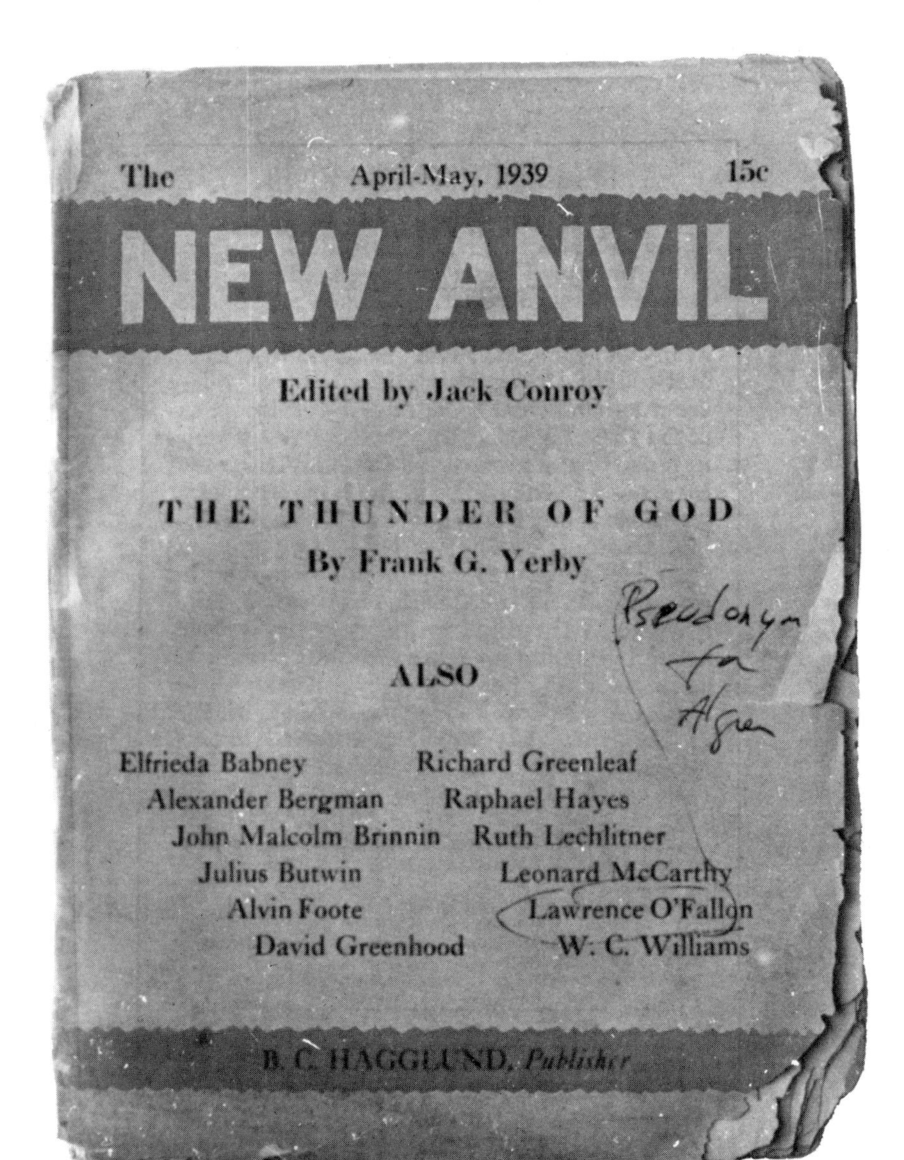
The New Anvil magazine cover, reproduced as an image:

The April-May, 1939 15c

NEW ANVIL

Edited by Jack Conroy

THE THUNDER OF GOD
By Frank G. Yerby

ALSO

Elfrieda Babney
Alexander Bergman
John Malcolm Brinnin
Julius Butwin
Alvin Foote
David Greenhood
Richard Greenleaf
Raphael Hayes
Ruth Lechlitner
Leonard McCarthy
Lawrence O'Fallon
W. C. Williams

B. C. HAGGLUND, *Publisher*

Nelson Algren served as Managing Editor of *The New Anvil,* published bimonthly from Chicago and printed in San Benito, Texas. (The first issue was printed in Pelly, Texas.) This issue contained a poem by Algren printed as a joke under the name of a friend, Lawrence O'Fallon.

"Makers of Music," *The New Anvil,* 1 (March 1939), 23.
Line nine in column two of this poem contains a misprint. It should read "Hopers from Home reading all about it" for *reaching.*

"Utility Magnate," *The New Anvil,* 1 (April-May 1939), 16.
Appeared under pen name Lawrence O'Fallon.

* "Program for Appeasement," *The New Anvil,* 1 (June-July 1939), 12.

"Home and Goodnight," *Poetry,* 55 (November 1939), 74.

"Travelog," *Poetry,* 55 (November 1939), 76.

"How Long Blues," *Poetry,* 58 (September 1941), 309.

"Local South," *Poetry,* 58 (September 1941), 308.

"The Swede Was a Hard Guy," *Southern Review,* 7 (1941-42), 873.

"Epitaph: The Man with the Golden Arm," *Poetry,* 70 (September 1947), 316.

"Nobody Knows," *The Saturday Review of Literature,* 49 (3 September 1966), 15.

"An Absconding Bookie and Four Other Poems," *Chicago Tribune Magazine* (8 October 1972), 28.

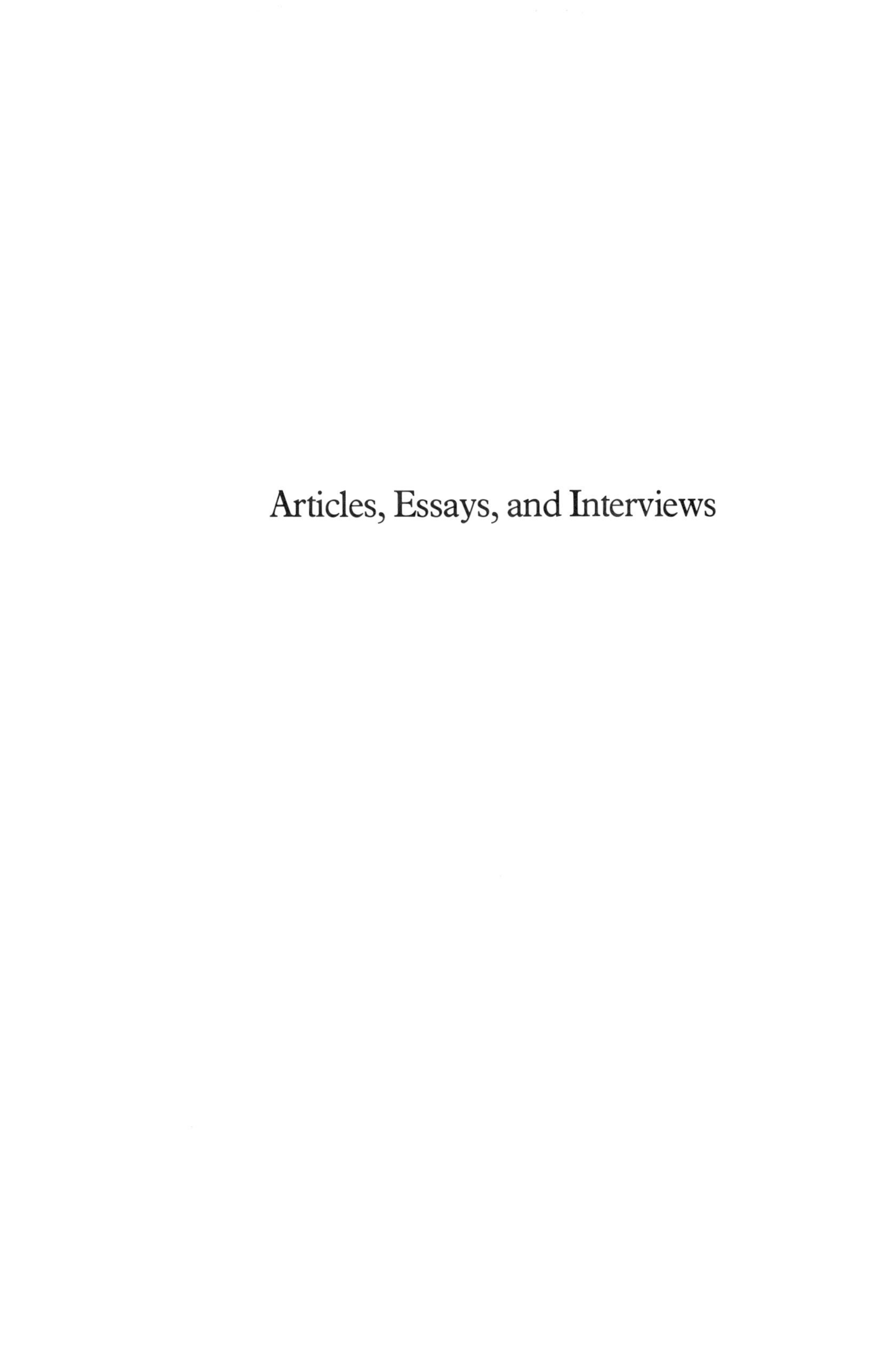

Articles, Essays, and Interviews

"'Politics' in Southern Illinois," *New Republic,* LXXIX (1 August 1934), 307. Unsigned article written by Algren.

"American Obituary," *Partisan Review,* II (October-November 1935), 26.

"Lloyd Frankenberg's Poems," *Poetry,* 56 (April 1940), 46.

"Do It the Hard Way," *The Writer,* 56 (March 1943), 67.

"Varying Viewpoints," *Poetry,* 57 (April 1943), 50.

* "Merry Christmas Mr. Mark," *Chicago Sunday Tribune,* Part 4 (4 December 1949), 3.

"What is America Reading?" *Northwestern University Reviewing Stand,* 13 (29 January 1950). Printed version of radio panel discussion.

* "Things of Earth: A Groundhog's View," *Pacific Citizen* (19 December 1952).

"American Christmas, 1952," *Nation,* 175 (27 December 1952), 2.

"Hollywood Djinn with a Dash of Bitters," *Nation,* 177 (25 July 1953), 68.

"Eggheads Are Rolling: The Rush to Conform," *Nation,* 177 (17 October 1953), 306.

* "8 'Angry Ones' Declare a British Existentialism," *Chicago Sunday Sun-Times,* Section 3 (13 April 1958), 1.

"Chicago is a Wose," *Nation,* 188 (28 February 1959), 191.

"A Talk on the Wild Side," *The Reporter,* 20 (11 June 1959), 31. Interview by David Ray.

* "Nelson Algren Writes Impressions of the [World] Series," *Chicago Sunday Sun-Times* (3 October 1959), 5.

* "Nelson Algren's Reflections: Hep-Ghosts of the Rain," *Chicago Sunday Sun-Times* (10 October 1959), 12.

* "The Mafia of the Heart," *Contact,* 6 (October 1960), 9.

"Down with All Hands," *Atlantic Monthly,* 206 (December 1960), 76. Travel article later in *Who Lost an American?*

"Remembering Richard Wright," *Nation,* 192 (28 January 1961), 85.

"The South of England," *Rogue,* 6 (May 1961), 26. Travel article later in *Who Lost an American?*

"The Peseta with the Hole in the Middle" (Part I), *Kenyon Review,* XXIII (Autumn 1961), 549. Travel article later in *Who Lost an American?*

"You Have Your People and I Have Mine," *Rogue,* 6 (November 1961), 28. Travel article on Ireland later in *Who Lost an American?*

"Hemingway: The Dye That Did Not Run," *Nation,* 193 (18 November 1961), 387.

"The Peseta with the Hole in the Middle" (Part II), *Kenyon Review,* XXIV (Winter 1962), 110. Travel article on Seville later in *Who Lost an American?*

"The Moon of King Minos," *Rogue,* 7 (February 1962), 26. Travel article on Crete later in *Who Lost an American?*

"Fabulous Istanbul Isn't the Town for Me," *Nugget,* VII (June 1962), 31. Travel article on Istanbul later in *Who Lost an American?*

"Dad Among the Troglogodites or, Show Me a Gypsy and I'll Show You a Nut," *Noble Savage,* 5 (October 1962), 59. Travel article on Almería later in *Who Lost an American?*

"The Father and Son Cigar," *Playboy,* 9 (December 1962), 97. Travel article on Chicago later in *Who Lost an American?*

"Shlepker, or White Goddess Say You Not Go That Part of Forest," *Cavalier,* 13 (February 1963), 12. Travel article later in *Notes from a Sea Diary: Hemingway All the Way.*

* "Whobody Knows My Name, or How To Be a Freedom-Rider Without Leaving Town," *Harlequin* (April 1963), 8. Travel article on New York from *Who Lost an American?*

"Nelson Algren Interviewed: The Writer as Child, Youth and Army Privateer," *The Carleton Miscellany,* IV (Fall 1963), 3. Interview by H.E.F. Donohue later in *Conversations with Nelson Algren.*

"Ginger Man Who Couldn't," *Nation,* 198 (6 April 1964), 351.

"Un-American Idea: Sex Can Be Funny," *Life,* 56 (8 May 1964), 8.

"The Donkeyman by Twilight," *Nation,* 198 (18 May 1964), 509.

"Who's Who at the Lost and Found," *Nation,* 198 (1 June 1964), 560.

"The Radical Innocent," *Nation,* 199 (21 September 1964), 142.

"Nelson Algren at Fifty-Five," *Atlantic Monthly,* 214 (October 1964), 79. Interview by H.E.F. Donohue — excerpts from *Conversations with Nelson Algren.*

* "Hemingway All the Way," *Cavalier* (February 1965), 30.

"The Question of Simone de Beauvoir," *Harper's,* 230 (May 1965), 135.

"Simone a Go Go," *Ramparts,* 4 (October 1965), 65.

"Down with Cops," *Saturday Evening Post,* CCXXXVIII (23 October 1965), 10.

"I Know They'll Like Me in Cholon," *The Critic,* XXVII (February-March 1969), 58.

"They Don't Belong to Us," *The Critic,* XXVII (November-December 1969), 58.

"The Rest of the Way Is by the Stars," *Chicago Free Press,* 1 (5 October 1970), 22. Algren was a contributing writer on the staff of the *Chicago Free Press.*

"A Ticket to Biro-Bidjan," *Chicago Free Press,* 1 (5 October 1970), 37.

"Early Chicago Journalism," *Chicago Free Press,* 1 (12 October 1970), 28.

"Previous Days," *Chicago Free Press,* 1 (19 October 1970), 30.

"The Cop Mentality," *Chicago Free Press,* 1 (9 November 1970), 27.

* "White Mice and Mama-sans Take It All," *Rolling Stone,* No. 83 (27 May 1971), 30.

"No Cumshaw, No Rickshaw" (Part 1), *Holiday,* 49 (July-August 1971), 32.

"No Cumshaw, No Rickshaw" (Part 2), *Holiday,* 50 (November 1971), 44.

"Where Did Everybody Go?" *Chicago Tribune Magazine* (13 February 1972), 20.

"Blanche Sweet Under the Tapioca," *Chicago Tribune Magazine* (30 April 1972), 42.

"The Way to Médenine," *Playboy,* 19 (December 1972), 153.

"The Word Game," *The Critic,* XXXI (January-February 1973), 74. Reprinted as "The Six Best Novels of World War II, and Why Five Died," *Intellectual Digest,* III (April 1973), 68.

"Some blunt but not unkind words from Nelson Algren," *Chicago Sun-Times* (26 March 1973), 14.

Reviews

Review of *A World to Win,* by Jack Conroy. *The Windsor Quarterly,* II (Fall 1935), 73.

Review of *Judgment Day,* by James T. Farrell. *The Windsor Quarterly,* II (Fall 1935), 83.

"Sentiment with Terror," *Poetry,* 55 (December 1939), 157. *Collected Poems,* by Robert Graves.

"Spiritual Victory of a Poet," *Chicago Sunday Sun-Times* (9 May 1949), 40. *Limbo Tower,* by William Greshen.

Review of *The Golden Spike,* by Hal Ellson. *The Saturday Review of Literature,* XXXV (6 December 1952), 35.

"City Against Itself," *Nation,* 178 (13 February 1954), 135. *Big Bill of Chicago,* by Lloyd Wendt.

"Bitter Physics of the Deprived," *The Saturday Review of Literature,* 36 (4 July 1954), 21. *Duke,* by Hal Ellson.

"Dreiser Hedged Out," *Nation,* 188 (16 May 1959), 459. *Letters of Theodore Dreiser,* by Robert H. Elias.

"Junkie Beware," *Nation,* 194 (3 February 1962), 106. *The Drug Experience,* by David Ebin.

"Raising Cain in the Corn Field," *Book Week* (31 October 1965), 4. *With the Procession,* by Henry B. Fuller; *Windy McPherson's Son,* by Sherwood Anderson; and *Gullible's Travels,* by Ring W. Lardner.

"Close Call," *Book Week* (6 February 1966), 12. *My Escape from the CIA,* by Hughes Rudd.

"Between Dream and Waking," *The Critic,* XXVI (December 1967-January 1968), 71. *A Story That Ends with a Scream and Eight Others,* by James Leo Herlihy.

"Native Son," *The Critic,* XXVI (June-July 1968), 66. *Richard Wright,* by Constance Webb.

"Tricky Dickey," *The Critic,* XXVII (May-June 1970), 77. *Deliverance,* by James Dickey.

"How to Break Silence Conspiracy over Old Age," *Los Angeles Times Book Review* (25 June 1972), 1. *The Coming of Age,* by Simone de Beauvoir.

Review of *Ringolevio: A Life Played for Keeps,* by Emmett Grogan. *The Critic,* XXXI (September-October 1972), 87.

Review of *The World of Apples,* by John Cheever. *Chicago Tribune Book World* (13 May 1973), 1.

"A Convocation of Vonnegut Characters," *Los Angeles Times Book Review* (10 June 1973), 3. *Breakfast of Champions,* by Kurt Vonnegut, Jr.

"The Great Hemorrhoid Hunt or Kiss-Kiss Bang-Bang Goes Arty-Arty," *The Critic,* XXXI (July-August 1973), 6. *Last Tango in Paris* (movie).

Published Letters

To Erling Larsen, *The Carleton Miscellany,* VI (Winter 1965), 104.

To Joe Wells, *The Critic,* XXV (February-March 1967), 20 and cover. On young Americans making a cult of neo-Nazi paraphernalia.

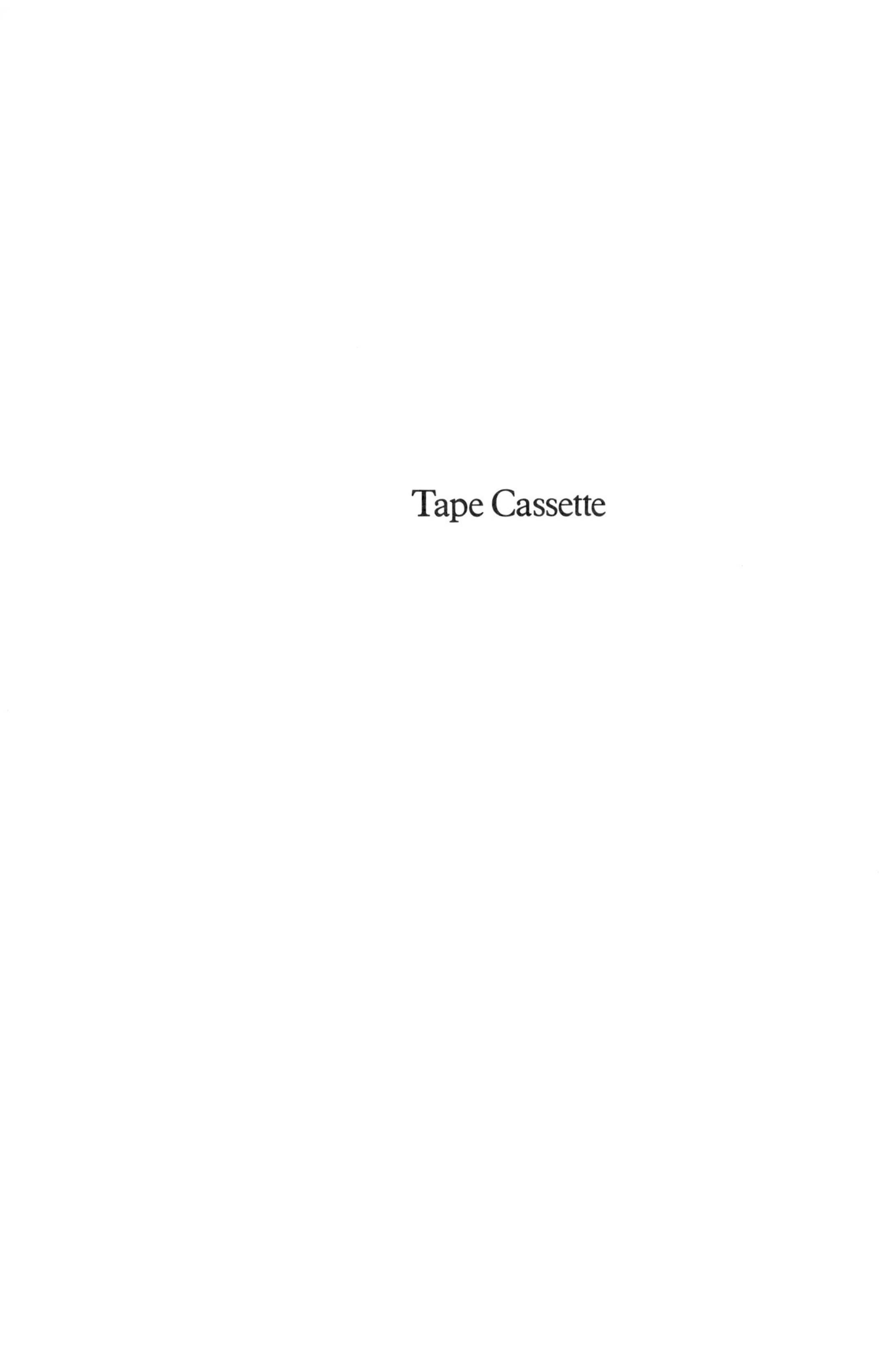

Tape Cassette

Dark Came Early in That Country. Chicago: Thomas More Association, 1973. Mediatape # M-120. Nelson Algren reads story excerpts and poetry, including: "Home to Shawneetown," "Ode to an Absconding Bookie," "I Never Hollered Cheezit the Cops," "Epitaph: The Man with the Golden Arm," and others.

References

nelson algren samuel beckett. Columbus, Ohio: Ohio State University Libraries, [1966].
This booklet lists works shown at an exhibition of books and manuscripts selected from the Ohio State University Libraries collections in November 1966.

Appendix
WPA Manuscript

Note: The following revised typescript fragment of "Salomon and Morris: Two Patriots of the Revolution" was one of Algren's WPA assignments sometime between 1936 and 1939. According to Algren it was done for the B'nai B'rith or some similar organization and was probably never published. Page 20 is missing and the typescript breaks off at page 22.

Of his tour of duty with the WPA, Algren reminisces:

> I used to get fired every six weeks regularly by John T. Frederick. He kept assuring me I'd be happier off the Project and hand me a 403. Then I'd find I was happier on it. So I'd go down to the relief station again, register as a pauper, receive a sack of moldy potatoes; and materialize the following morning in the Project office.*

* Jerre Mangione, *The Dream and the Deal: The Federal Writers Project 1935-1943* (Boston: Little, Brown, 1972), p. 121.

WPA STUFF

Salomon and Morris: Two Patriots of the Revolution

"Land tolerating all, accepting all - " -Whitman

In the year 1772 a penniless Pole fresh from Lissa was trying to learn English along the wharves of New York: a poor boy doing the best he could. He learned languages swiftly - but before he knew English well he was sitting in a British prison for conspiring against the king. He had associated himself with an underground order called the Sons of Liberty. And so sat, in his frayed clothes, his sense of humor flattered at being so chosen as a menace to the empire.

His name was Haym Salomon: and a greater menace he was to become. Greater than the Empire itself could have dreamed. Learning of his facility with languages, his captors released him in order to obtain his services as an interpreter among their Hessian mercenaries. Imperial regret at so sparing the little man was to come later. His function among the Hessians became, gradually, less that of the interpreter than that of the agitator.

He sensed the unspoken resentment of these German youths at being sold like cattle into the English service, to be shipped four thousand miles to fight a people as poor as themselves. Their heart was not in the fighting. Salomon told them of Washington's offer of a hundred acres of good land to every Hessian who deserted to the American ranks. A Hessian might answer then that Salomon lied, that only a baron could own so much land.

But it was hard not to believe this Salomon in anything: one had only to watch his eyes when he said such things to know he did not lie. He gave them further assurance: "And a hundred acres more as soon as you can plow them."

That often sowed a proper seed. Desertions occurred wherever the reticent little immigrant wandered in the city. On the night of August 5, 1778, the Empire knocked again at his door.

He sent his wife into the bedroom to care for the baby, and when she came out she caught a glimpse of him, behind a British flare and a British drum, surrounded by redcoats making a small parade of their prisoner through the narrow New York streets to the Provost Jail.

2.

The Provost was the most sinister of all Britain's sinister prisons. Salomon had witnessed the hanging of a schoolteacher named Nathan Hale here; it must have been a consolation to him to feel that, like Hale, he too was giving his life for a country truly his own. But whether it was his own as fully as it had been the schoolteacher's or not, he was going to hang for it all the same. He had evaded them once. Now it was one fate for spies, and that with speed and no mercy.

Salomon was shoved into a drafty, filth-ridden room on the second floor, reserved for American officers and more or less distinguished prisoners. A survivor of that room wrote, after the Revolution, that it was so overcrowded that when men lay down to sleep they had to lie packed like sardines clear across the room from wall to wall, so tightly that, when bones ached beyond endurance, one would cry out the command, "Right to left- turn!" And the whole compact mass would turn together. In derision the prison overseer, one Cunningham, had named this room Congress Hall.

The drum-head court-martial did not take place in the Provost, but in flat-faced red brick building facing upper New York Bay.

He was charged with using his home to assist the escape of Continental prisoners.

He was charged with sheltering spies.

He was charged with communicating with Americans.

He was charged with being an accessory to a plot to burn the King's fleet in the Harbor of New York.

He was charged with using his capacity as an interpreter for the Hessian troops to promote desertion and sedition.

He was charged with treason.

In short, they threw the book at him.

Perhaps they told him he should have gone back where he came from. Then

3.

hanged he was sentenced to be.

His guard, one writer asserts[1], was a big, goodnatured Hessian youth whom Salomon had earlier befriended by gifts of snuff. What passed between them, in the long hours, is matter for conjecture. He owned a Swiss watch that may have served to bribe the boy. It may have been that Alexander MacDougall, firebrand organizer of the Sons of Liberty, effected his release. At any rate, both guard and prisoner were gone by morning.

Salomon literally wormed his way through the British lines for days, hiding in brush at the sound of a horse's hooves or the turn of a twig, until he made the American lines. A Dutch farmer named Vanhelb helped him when he was lost. A lieutenant named Gregory greeted him when he entered the Continental lines .

He remained a short time within the American encampment in an effort to lose a cough he had contracted in the Provost. With one hand against his chest he stood watching the ragged Continentals drill.

Not one of the rank and file was uniformed. They wore old pantaloons,hand-me-down breeches, anything and everything. Those who owned hats thrust green twigs into them to display some sort of uniformity. Others pinned white rags across their chests and around their legs; a comic-opera army with bent and rusted bayonets. Salomon wondered how an army so poor was able to stay in the field at all.

He perceived that the nation's most formidable enemy was bankruptcy: as he watched them drill, himself as ragged as any man of them, he told himself that the war would ultimately be won or lost in the counting houses, Britain might not beat these men in the field; but Britain could starve them out of the ranks.

Salomon formed a new picture of the Revolution in his mind:The men in the armies were only one aspect of the struggle. The Continental Congress was another facet. The farmers, the workers, the mechanics of America were another. And all three lined with a single chain :

1 Mr. Howard Fast, in Haym Salomon and the Revolution.

4.

Money.

Without it the men would not stay in the field a month; without it the Congress would collapse. Without it the Revolution would fail.

England's king hit the nail on the head when he is said to have remarked, about this time, "My one true ally is the rebel's money--or their lack of it." He assured his ministers that the war would end when the colonies could no longer clothe and feed their troops, and his optimism was only too well founded. American money was a joke laughed at by all the world, even by the Americans themselves. One silver dollar was worth 525 paper dollars. Paper money was used to burn Tory homes and to decorate Whig interiors. Bundles of notes were given mock burials accompanied by dirges and orations. Philadelphia merchants marched through the streets wearing bills as cockades, accompanied by a tarred hound into whose hide bills had been set. Workmen lost their wages even while earning them, and the government itself was in much the same condition. When it attempted taxation it was snowed under by its own paper and was legally powerless to enforce its effort.

Not even knowing the whereabouts of his wife and son with certainty, Solomon was reckless enough of his own chances to assume that he had not yet done enough for his adopted land. His own clothes were in tatters, but he was going to uniform an army; he didn't know where his next meal was coming from, but he was going to find food for a nation's soldiery. And if, as a Jew, he could not, officially, stabilize a nation's currency, then he would do that through the man whose official responsibility it was. He began walking the long and perilous hundred miles to Philadelphia, turning over his knowledge of foreign exchange in his mind:

5.

there was probably no one in the world who knew as much about foreign exchange at that time as did this self-effacing sloe-eyed hitchhiker bumming his solitary way through the colonial wilderness.

In Philadelphia he found his family. The city was still held by the [illegible] rebels and most of the colonies' Jews were now living there, having fled New York when the British had taken that city. When New York had fallen the capital had been removed to Philadelphia. Since that time Philadelphia's commerce had become the most vigorous in the nation, till America's very life had come to depend upon the commerce of this single city. Salomon had come to a place which would give his talents their greatest opportunity and their largest exercise.

With the assistance of one Jacob Ben Casro he gained a foothold as a broker in the coffee house exchanges of Front Street, where he built himself a reputation for unimpeachable honesty and unequalled perceptions. His influence, in time, so modified Philadlephia's daily buying and selling that he became, in a sense, himself that city's commerce. The manner in which he exercised this influence is illustrated by an incident which occurred while the government was attempting to buy flour on the Philadelphia exchange. All day the market had been engineered silently by Salomon. All that could be sensed was that Salomon was buying and selling flour, buying and selling. Every time he sold, it seemed, for some reason, that the price had been shaved down.

"Salomon says don't hold flour", the word went around. And Salomon's word was suffieient. The government agent probably never learned precisely who his ally was that day, for Salomon did such things with as little display as possible. The agent did know, when that day's selling was done, that the government had been saved four thousand dollars.

6

His assistance was usually more direct, and it was not confined to the American forces. The French Legions of Armand and Lafayette were assisted out of his private purse, according to Charles Edward Russell, Salomon's biographer. And as the bitter years dragged on, with the British coming to depend more and more upon their economic blockade and less and less upon their Hessians and Redcoats, the number of key revolutionists depending upon Salomon's personal bounty increased.

Baron Von Steuben, who arrived in time to give new vigor to Washington's freezing regiments at Valley Forge, was one. And a young delegate from Virginia by name of James Madison wrote to a friend:

> I cannot in any way make you more sensible to the importance of your kind attention to pecuniary remittances for me than by informing you that I have for some time been a pensioner on the favor of Haym Salomon, a Jew broker.

Not long after, to the same friend, the tone was changed.

> The kindness of our little friend in Front Street near the coffee house, is a fund that will prevent me from extremities, but I never resort to it without great mortification, as he obstinately rejects all recompense. The price of money is so usorious that he thinks it ought to be extracted from none but those that aim at profitable speculation. To a necessitous delegate he gratitously spares a supply out of his private stock.

By 1780 Philadelphia had become a pauper capital of a pauper nation. In the bitter winter of that year its streets were filled with the poor and the place-seekers: the people were suffering. The maimed and the homeless waited on charity: returning veterans, sick or well,

7

had to shift for themselves. Deservers and undeservers, petitioner and profiteer, jack-tar and mechanic, all put in their claims for food and shelter and warmth and work..

The government could scarcely feed and clothe its armies, far less its city masses. What was given had to come from individuals.

Salomon gave. Without ostentation. "He gave without stint," one writer observes, "and without putting shame in the hearts of those who asked." When his money ran low he sold real estate and personal property. He gave to both the high and the lowly.

Don Francesco Rendon, Royal Emissary of his most Christian Majesty, the King of Spain, arrived to tell the colonies that, although his king could not assist directly, he would be pleased to help indirectly. But the Don's funds went astray, and he was shortly hard put to maintain his dignity as a royal messenger. He was told that, if his message was relevant to the American cause, he should find his way to the coffee house on Front Street between Market and Arch.

He found his way: in the shadowed rear Salomon was conducting business as paymaster to the French forces and broker to the French Consul. The Don was placed on the little men's bounty, illustrating that it was not necessary to be a member of Congress to receive Salomon's help.

Nor was it necessary to be a Don. Soldiers from the ranks were pensioned by him as well, Men from whom he could never expect any manner of personal return. Others constitute a list that reads like a register of our early history. Among the better remembered were

8

General Mifflin, later governor of Pennsylvania; General Arthur St. Clair, first governor of the Northwest Territory; General Charles Lee, close in command to Washington; Joseph Reed, secretary to Washington and one of the heroes of Brandywine and Monmouth; John Paul Jones; James Monroe; the Marquis Charles Armand Taffin, a French aristocrat whose cavalry did yeoman service for Washington; Joseph Jones, one of the oldest members of Congress; James Wilson; later a justice of the Supreme Court; Daniel Morgan, hero of the Cowpens; Edmund Randolph, First Secretary of State; Thomas Jefferson, Thaddous Kosciusko; Theodoric Bland, a great-great grandson of Pocahontas and captain of the First Troop of Virginia Horse; Major William McPherson, commander of a partisan corps of cavalry; and Benjamin Lincoln, Secretary of War and the man who received the sword of Cornwallis at Yorktown.

The Superintendent of Finance was also an immigrant. Born in a Liverpool slum and come to America at thirteen, he had so prospered that by 1775 he was the colonies' wealthiest merchant. On a warm April day of that year he stood before a hundred Philadelphia business leaders celebrating St. George's Day by reaffirming his allegiance to the crown. Most of the merchants were not reassured by his reaffirmation. They recalled a day in 1765 when an English vessel loaded with stamp paper had appeared off Gloucester Point.

Ships in the harbor had lowered their flags to half-mast.

Drums muffled in black crepe had been beaten up and down the streets by giant Negroes, to signify the death of liberty.

Commoners armed with flaming torches had gathered in the public square.

And the chairman had gone to the home of a shopkeeper appointed to sell the stamps and hinted blandly that the shopkeeper's home might be torn down stone by stone and the shopkeeper murdered into the bargain, were the stamps sold. Later this Morris had joined with radicals in calling for a total boycott of English goods.

Who didn't know of his common heritage?

That his grandfather had been a "tar" and that his father had worked in an iron mill?

Hadn't there been talk, too, of an illegitimate half-brother? The father had left £500 to the woman in his will, shamelessly admitting her existence.

His listeners must have concluded that, despite the chairman's

·7

eloquence, they were being deceived. Before that April day was over, news arrived that Continentals had already engaged the British at Lexington. Most of the business men hurried to their homes, some to barricade themselves from the "Revolutionary rabble." Those that remained in the hall were known revolutionists. At the head of the table sat Morris. They gathered around him to plan their parts in the struggle ahead.

The Tories knew at last where Robert Morris stood.

Yet such was this man's nature that the following year the very men among whom he had cast his lot found cause to doubt him as much as had his Tory associates.

On July 2, 1776, Congressmen of the embattled colonies were voting on a resolution for an outright declaration of independence. Jefferson, a young delegate from Virginia, after conceding point after point, after rewriting and diluting sentence after sentence, finally lost all patience and declared: "This document shall stand or fall in its present form!"

When the resolution was carried, among those who voted against it was Robert Morris, delegate from Pennsylvania. According to one story, as he left the hall with three other Pennsylvanians who had also voted against the measure, Ben Franklin called him aside and dryly suggested that he could best serve his country by staying at home, on July 4, when the formal signing of the document would take place.

p. 10

Tom Paine, majority leader in the Pennsylvania legislature, demanded the immediate recall of three of those who had voted against the Declaration. But even Morris' worst enemies admitted that he was a man who would do what he thought was right though it cost him his neck. The Revolution needed such men. Morris kept his job and eventually signed the document. Later he explained: "I have opposed the Declaration of Independence because in my poor opinion it was an improper time and will neither promote the interest nor rebound to the honor of America." This would indicate that Morris' concern and hope for America's future was an economic concern and an economic hope.

But those who felt that, in spite of everything, the Revolution needed him were soon confirmed in their judgement.

Howe, advancing rapidly on the stricken colonies, prepared to attack Philadelphia, seat of the central government. The congress fled to Baltimore after asking Morris and two others to stay behind and strengthen the city's defenses. Christmas was a few days off and the people of Philadelphia had begun decorating their homes for the holiday. Then--in a manner still in fashion--Tories spread false rumors that Howe had surrounded the city and was advancing on all sides.

Within a few hours the snow-bound roads were jammed with refugees and by nightfall the city was deserted except for the soldiers and a band of workmen under the Morris' supervision. Even Morris' assistants fled.

Morris supervised the construction of barricades. He paid the

8-11

men bonuses out of his own purse. He worked at their side on the docks, and when the work proceeded slowly he wrote: "Our people knew not the hardships and calamities of war when they so boldly dared Britain to arms."

On Christmas night Washington and a small band of half-frozen soldiers crossed the ice-packed Delaware to surprise the Hessians at Trenton. The British began retreating all along the line. The strategy of Washington and the stubborn courage of Robert Morris had saved the capital from external attack. Meanwhile, the city's economic life had been perserved by a thousand devices of one Haym Salomon.

In the critical months before Yorktown Salomon worked most closely with Morris. Both felt the struggle developing into a crisis, and both threw their every resource, their every energy, behind Washington. Although Morris did not appoint Salomon officially as Broker to the Office of the Superintendent of Finance until March 6, 1782, he had leaned upon Salomon, unofficially, in that capacity, from the beginning of the struggle. Now he leaned upon him officially, in order to see Washington through. Salomon's interest was never higher--when he took anything--than one-fourth of one percent. Literally, he was our first dollar-a-year man. Morris' developing dependence upon him is recorded with monotonous frequency in the latter's diary:

"I sent for Salomon."

"I sent for Mr. Salomon."

"I sent for Haym Salomon."

"I sent for Salomon."

The invaders held the South. They held New York; they blockaded the coast. they retained the loyalty of a considerable section of the population. Those that struggled for a republic had to seek out the Tories within their lines as well as keep two armies in the field. Their struggle can be likened to that of Spanish Republicans in our own time. As in Spain, it brought freedom-loving men from all over the world to aid the fight for democracy: Lafayette, Von Steuben, Kosciusko and De Kalb. A singular difference was that in America the armies were controlled by a Congress possessing no power to tax. There was no legal means of getting money either for the regular armies or for the legions of such men as named above. The war behind the lines became a war for money.

Money for medicine, money for food, money for arms, money to pay members of Congress, to pay officers and enlisted men, to pay an army of clerks, to buy blankets, shoes, clothes, to pay interest on loans, to pay loans due, to buy saddles, to buy horses, loans and loans and yet more loans.

Two majors addressed a threatening letter to Morris, demanding money.

He answered:

Gentlemen:

I have received this morning your application. I

-13-

make the earliest answer to it. You demand instant payment. I have no money to pay you with. Your most obedient and humble servant.

Robert Morris

Washington divulged to Morris a daring hope to move most of his army across several hundred miles of open country, in complete secrecy, to attack Cornwallis at Yorktown, and Morris took the responsibility of assuring him that he would finance the movement-- and returned to Philadelphia "scarcely able to breathe with excitement." Salomon floated about $200,000 worth of government securities, and Morris sent 300 barrels of flour, 300 barrels of salt meat, 10 hogsheads of rum, and boats to carry 7,000 men.

Washington asked him for money to purchase enemy information, Morris sent $400.

Washington asked for money to pay his men a bonus.

Morris sent $50,000.

He found time to build up a fleet of seven small vessels to harry British shipping. One of these darted through the blockade to bring blankets, muskets, and powder into port.

He pleaded and threatened state legislatures for money to pay the troops. But the money did not come, and Washington wrote wistfully: "The services they are going on are disagreeable to the Northern regiments but I make no doubt that a douceur of a little hard money would put them in proper temper." Morris thereupon borrowed $20,000 in his own name. As Washington approached Yorktown, still undiscovered,

-14-

Morris confided to his diary that he could neither eat nor sleep. While the army moved, there was no rest.

Harassed as he was, he chose this moment, to found, with such men as Hamilton, a national bank. While the army moved he addressed the King of France to suggest that, if America went under for lack of funds, France would find herself allied to a lost cause. When Amsterdam bankers requested collateral, Morris replied with eloquent assurances of America's future. The Dutch and French complained that Morris treated kings and ministers like "common cashiers." But both feared the prospect of a victorious Britain. Thus arrived, from France, "Le Resolute," bearing 2,500,224 livres. The money was rushed to the new bank--The Bank of America--in Philadelphia, which, within the following two weeks, loaned the United States $100,000.

On the morning of Nov. 3, 1781, Morris and the French Minister stood among a few hundred poorly dressed and undernourished men and women facing a crudely painted altar of a small Catholic church. While a white frocked boys' choir sang, the flags of England, France, and the United States were borne through the door by Continental soldiers. Cornwallis had surrendered. The invasion was crushed.

Yet the war was not over. There was still a fifth column to contend with: those who had staked their fortunes on a British victory and would not accept a victory by farmers, armed with ancient muskets, over the earth's mightiest empire. Somewhere in this new and impossible aggregation of colonies, calling themselves "states" they felt, was an Achilles heel.

There was, and they found it. Morris had converted the Bank's funds into soldier's pay and flour, into bullets and shoes. Depositors received anonymous letters warning them that Morris had cheated them and that they would never see a dime of their money. In a crowd an unidentified voice would suddenly cry out: "Ask Robert Morris to show you your money. He cannot."

A run on the bank began and back into coffee pots and mattresses went the life blood of the almost-achieved Revolution. Frantic cashiers sent for Morris, and Morris put on a show.

He scattered silver everywhere: on every counter, across the floor. Sweating workmen carted the gleaming metal in and out of the vaults from morning till night. A chain of silver led from wall to wall and from door to door. The merchants brought their money back though the vaults were empty, though each piece of silver had been shown to them in a dozen different places.

After the war Morris returned to private life to rebuild his depleted fortune. He invested heavily in European bonds, bonds rendered worthless by the sudden rise of Napoleon. He bought land, and the land proved to be a swamp. His ships were lost at sea, his warehouses were destroyed by fire. Creditors began clamoring, and he was jailed for a debt of a few hundred dollars. On the night of February 16, 1789, he entered a debtors' prison. He wrote in his diary that he, who was once America's richest man, now owned the flour and spice in his pantry, an

-16

¶

old carriage, the clothes on his back, and a watch that had belonged to his father.

After serving three and a half years, Morris was released still owing three million dollars. Gouverneur Morris provided his wife with a small pension, and the one time Superintendent of Finance spent his last years in a frame cottage in Philadelphia's poorest section.

No two men holding such responsible posts were so quickly forgotten after their deaths as were Salomon and Morris. Almost a century passed before the first biography appeared of Morris--the man Washington called "Perhaps the most responsible for our success." For the business end of any war is grubbing and unpopular: people must be taxed, creditors must be stalled off, money must be borrowed. And the men whose job it is to supply the guns are usually not heroic figures. Certainly the stout, phlegmatic Morris was not heroic to the eye. And no one remembered that, when the decisive hour arrived, this man, against the interests of his class, cast his lot with those who fought for democracy and freedom.

* * *

Haym Salomon barely outlived the cause for which he had fought. If he anticipated any official recognition of his services when the new government was organized, he must have been sadly disillusioned. No Jew was offered a place in this new government.

In partnership with one Jacob Mordecai, therefore, he opened a house at 22 Wall Street and advertised that he would there operate as a broker and dealer in bank stocks. The Philadelphia house on Front Street was put up for sale, since he planned to bring his family to New York as soon as the firm was established. ~~But although he made several trips to New York, he never lived there again.~~ Jacob Mordecai soon found that Salomon's former interest in business maneuvering was lagging. Now that the war was done, his attention wandered: when he came to New York it was, apparently, chiefly to linger around the Battery talking to old skippers, privateers and blockade-runners. His services, and the hacking cough of the Provost, were tiring him: he did not have it left in him, now, to seek a personal fortune. Since the nation was free, he no longer felt the immediate daily necessity for turning worthless paper into hard gold. What for? He wrote to Morris saying that he felt it a man's duty to leave his sons a legacy of liberty rather than money or land or goods.

That was, shortly, all he was to leave a wife and four children. Apparently he formulated no plans whatsoever for recovering any part of the sums he had expended, directly and indirectly, to the government and to individuals.

Yet he must have known that he was not to live long. To his friend and assistant, McRae, he had confided his condition. When he could no longer conceal the seriousness of his cough, he returned to Philadelphia and to Rachel. He lay in bed waiting death, and he did not have to wait long. The end came peacefully. On January 7, 1785, he was buried in Philadelphia's old Jewish burying ground. Rachel was

left penniless, with two sons and two daughters to raise.

"All Americans of all races may acclaim Haym Salomon a Patriot," Prof. Albert Busnell Hart of Harvard University suggests, "a benefactor to his country, an inciter of patriotism to members of his race, to his countrymen of all races, and to later generations."

"He, undoubtedly, was a great patriot, " says Franklin D. Roosevelt "and rendered fine and unselfish service to the land of his adoption-- Our Nation."

Herbert Hoover has commented: "The noble and disinterested public services of Haym Salomon deserve the undying gratitude of all Americans. The aid of his financial genius and his wealth was of critical importance in the Revolutionary struggle which created us a nation."

The late Calvin Coolidge observed: "There is romance in the story of Haym Salomon, Polish Jew, financier of the Revolution.... He negotiated for Robert Morris all the loans raised in France and Holland, pledged his personal faith and fortune for enormous amounts, and personally advanced large sums to such men as James Madison, Thomas Jefferson, Baron Steuben, General St. Clair, and many other patriot leaders, who testified that without his aid they could not have carried on in the cause."

William Howard Taft said of him: ". . . a man entitled to the gratitude of the entire country."

No official recognition has yet been taken either of the country's financial or its moral debt to this man. Efforts to achieve both kinds

19—

of recognition have been stopped, time and time again. Sometimes the moment of application was inauspicious; sometimes records, substantiating claims, were found to have been lost or burned or stolen. Sometimes a bill seeking to honor the man's memory was quietly put to sleep.

In 1846 Haym M. Salomon, Salomon's son, being then sixty-one and living in adversity, applied to Congress for a part of the funds due his father's estate..

When the matter came up before the Committee on Revolutionary Claims of the Senate of the Twenty-ninth Congress, the committee unanimously adopted a report endorsing the claim and urging that it be paid.

This report came too late to be presented before the end of the session.

At the second session, the committee reverted to the claim and made another report on it that said:

". . . it appears from documentary evidence submitted by the memorialist that Haym Salomon, his father, contributed largely of his pecuniary means toward carrying on the war of the Revolution, aiding the public treasury by frequent loans of moneys and advancing liberally of his means to sustain many of the public men engaged in the struggle for independence at a time when the sinews of war were essential to success. It further appears to be satisfactorily established that the confidence of Mr. Salomon was so great in the good faith of the government that he parted with his money relying on that good faith for its return."

Before the next Congress, the Thirtieth, the claim was renewed

When Haym M. Salomon was in his seventies, he petitioned President Tyler for a tract of land in lieu of the country's indebtedness. The petition was approved. Then dropped.

Gestures toward compensating Salomon's heirs were again made at the 31st, 36th, 38th, and 39th Congress. But nothing came of them. Meanwhile, evidences of debt signed by Jefferson, Madison, Monroe, Miffin, Steuben, Wilson, vanished.

In 1893 the heirs, surrendering their claims, asked Congress for a medal in memory of Salomon. The 52nd Congress reported a bill appropriating $250 for a medal, but the bill failed of passage. In 1911 Woodrow Wilson, Louis Marshall and Governor Dix of New York collaborated in an effort to establish, with the aid of leading Jews, a memorial university in Salomon's name. Outbreak of the first world war killed that plan. In 1915 Wm. Howard Taft urged the building of a Salomon Memorial. Nothing happened. In 1918 Congressman Kahn proposed on the floor of the House some recognition of Salomon. Still no action. In 1925 Coolidge suggested something be done, and a bill was thereupon introduced, and failed of passage. Not even a proposal to make a public document of a biographical sketch of Salomon, offered in Congress in 1926, met with success.

On March 27, 1936, Congress passed a joint resolution authorizing the Secretary of the Interior to "grant permission for the erection on public grounds of the United States" in Washington a "memorial of proper and artistic form to the late Haym Salomon by his friends in

America in recognition of the patriotic and meritorious services rendered by him. . . ."

New York and Philadelphia have both contemplated monuments to Salomon, but in both instances plans miscarried. It is thus to Chicago's honor that the first successful attempt at recognition of the man should have been originated in this city, organized here, subscribed to by Chicagoans, and sculptered by Chicago artists.

The monument was conceived and first proposed by Mr. Barnet Hodes, Corporation Counsel of the city, not solely to commemorate a patriot, but to symbolize the republic's acceptance of all men, all creeds. The monument was subscribed to through the Patriotic Foundation of Chicago, an organization incorporated not for profit and having for its purpose acknowledgement of the conviction that peoples of all groups participated in the founding and building of this nation.

Funds were subscribed by popular subscription. Mayor Edward J. Kelly, in accepting the honorary chairmanship of the Foundation, heads the list of prominent supporters. Much of the aid which the project received came from Col. A. A. Sprague, co-chairman with Mr. Hodes, Ambassador Wm. E. Dodd, Dr. Charles Clayton Morrison of the Christian Century, A. D. Lasker, Dr. Walter Dill Scott, of Northwestern University, Laurence H. Armour, the late Maurice L. Rothchild, and Mrs. Fred Bernstein.

The working model of the monument was created by the late Lorado